THE ACTOR AND HIS AUDIENCE

W. A. Darlington

THE ACTOR AND HIS AUDIENCE

PHOENIX HOUSE

London

Contents

ILLUSTRATIONS

Author's Note

THERE ARE TWO MAIN WAYS OF SETTING OUT IN SEARCH OF A truth—the scientific and the imaginative. The scientific man assembles and establishes a mass of facts, and then deduces whether or not a principle is at work. The imaginative man first convinces himself that a principle must be at work, and then hunts about for factual evidence to prove its existence and its nature.

In this book I have had to use the second method because I am by temperament incapable of the first. The accumulation of small relevancies in which the research student delights is not for me. Faced with such a task, I find my faculties overpowered by inertia. I should make a pitiful historian, therefore, in the theatre or out of it. On the other hand I am confident, from a long experience in the theatre mostly in front of but sometimes behind the curtain, that in the actor-author relationship there is a principle at work, of great power and importance, the nature of which is not widely understood.

As a critic, who has gone to the theatre year after year three, four or five times a week, I have grown steadily more and more sensitive to the reactions of different audiences or different parts of the same audience. Without thinking about it, I know when the people about me in the stalls at first nights are applauding because they have enjoyed themselves, and when they are merely being polite to the management. The quantity of sound produced in each case may be the same, but its quality never.

As a dramatist, who has had the experience of seeing his own play night after night before different audiences, I have been able to find out for myself what I had only half understood from hearsay, how much the tempo of actors' performances, and therefore the atmosphere of a whole play, can vary according as an audience is quick or slow, warm or cold. Gradually I have reached the conviction that what is true of day-to-day variations in the temper of audiences in the same period must be equally true of variations from one period to another, and that those variations are much more important. To test this conviction by looking back into theatre history for evidence how actors and audiences had reacted upon one another in the past began to seem a task rewarding in itself and one which might perhaps prove something. Whether it has in fact proved anything is now for my readers to decide.

Throughout the book I have used historical detail only to serve my purpose, and with no regard to completeness. The biographical sketches of individual players, for instance, aim only at establishing what kind of man or woman each was, and what kind of player. I have selected such evidence as I needed from what came handiest, and as soon as I had enough to put my case clearly, I ceased to look for more. I have striven hard for accuracy, however, and, distrusting the effect of reported evidence, have sought for direct eye-witness accounts of the old actors wherever possible. In the task of checking these with their originals—grievous labour to one of my temperament if I had had to tackle it alone—I have been notably helped by the staff of my publishers, to whom I hereby offer my most grateful thanks.

I should also like to put on record my indebtedness to my friend and colleague, T. C. Kemp of Birmingham, who called my attention to the Garrick references in *Lichtenberg's Visits to England*, and lent me not only the book which contains them but also the rare Irving pamphlet *The Fashionable Tragedian*; to the Oxford University Press, publishers of the Lichtenberg volume, who gave me cordial permission to quote from it at considerable length; to Messrs Dent, who were equally kind over Gordon Craig's description of Irving in *The Bells;* and finally, to my fellow-members of the Garrick Club—to the Committee for allowing me to choose so many of my illustrations from the Club's collection, to the Secretary for his courtesy to my publishers when the reproductions were being made.

Chapter 1

THE ACTOR AS ARTIST

WHEN A MAN HAS BEEN A DRAMATIC CRITIC FOR MANY YEARS, people take it for granted that he must be an authority on acting. Hopeful young actors and actresses write to him in pathetic confidence that he can tell them how to set about their careers. When they have, with no help from him, taken the first steps on those careers, they write to him again, more in anger than in sorrow, demanding from him what they call Constructive Criticism. His job, they tell him, is not to dismiss their abortive efforts with slight regard, but to show them how to do better.

All this is nonsense. In the sense in which the term is used above, no dramatic critic is an authority on acting, or ought to be. He can only be such an authority in the light of his own experience; and no actor of experience can possibly be a good critic.

Neville Cardus, in his *Autobiography*, puts the case as it appears to the critic of music:

It is the absurdest convention of music criticism that it should pretend to estimate the technique of performance, a specialist's job. The music critic is not a teacher, not a voice producer, not an expert in what can be done with a piano, a fiddle, a trombone; his entire concern should be with his aesthetic reactions, and here he is (or should be) qualified by temperament and trained knowledge. I do not apologize for stating these elementary facts about the music critic's main job; they are to this day not generally understood among music purveyors.

And again:

From the moment I gave up ambitions towards executive ability in music, I was free to cultivate the art of listening—which is an art *sui generis*. The executant cannot hope often to listen to music and hear it in the absolute. The player in him, the performer . . . will interfere with the processes of reception.

My knowledge of music is negligible, but there is not a word in either of those extracts which I cannot understand and endorse from my parallel experience in the theatre. No actor can judge a play by its total effect, for he is always fatally distracted by his interest in the technical strokes by which the effect is built up. The

critic who allows himself to be so distracted is lost; and it is therefore not at all surprising that among the best of our dramatic
critics have been found men who could not even recognize the
technical strokes for what they were.

'I don't claim', one of these men said to me once, 'to know what
bad acting consists of, but I do know very well the effect that bad
acting has on me.' And he added, paraphrasing a remark of Dr.
Johnson's, that you do not have to be a hen to know whether
an egg is bad.

If, then, I set first my pen and subsequently my signature to a
book about acting, I should like the reader to understand clearly
from the start that I am writing not as an authority but as a
seeker after knowledge; that I am setting out not on a lecture tour
but a journey of discovery. Where it will take me I do not know.
Explorers seldom know where they are going until they arrive, and
are not at all disconcerted if, trying to find the back door of India,
they find themselves on the front doorstep of America. I can at
least promise myself an interesting new experience, for I have been
a regular playgoer for over forty years and a professional one for
nearly thirty, and have seen about five thousand plays in that time;
and yet in all those years I have hardly ever had serious occasion
to consider the actor except in relation to his setting and background. Devoted though I have always been to his art, and susceptible to his power, I have yet taken him for granted. Now I
must look at him in a new light and find out, if I can, what sort of
person he is. Through mere familiarity I have learnt that he is not
the godlike creature living in an enchanted world that I thought
him when I first fell under his spell. He is only a man now—but
a man not quite as other men. He is still a being set apart. And the
most cursory glance at his history shows that not merely here and
now, but at all times and in all lands, the actor has been set apart
from his fellows.

Sometimes this setting apart has been solidly established by
custom, or even by law. Custom in Japan used to decree that the
actors who played women's parts on the stage should live like
women off it, wearing the clothes of women and using their code
of manners. Law in England at one time classed the actor among
the rogues and vagabonds. Those days are gone, and to-day the
actor ranks as a member of an honourable and honoured profession, which recruits its numbers from every social class of the community, and attracts some of the most highly educated products

of the universities. The barrier which sets the actor apart is no longer visible or tangible; yet it is still there, undeniable and impassable as ever. The changes in the actor's social and professional standing have not made him less of a mystery.

It is a truism that every artist is something of a mystery to those who do not share his urge to express himself. But what cannot be imaginatively shared can still be intellectually grasped; and the man in the street can understand well enough that the artist has something to say and cannot be at rest until he has said it. Yet even a man who sees clearly what other artists are about may still be baffled by the actor. Between the ordinary man and the poet, the painter, the sculptor, the architect, or the musician (whether creative or interpretative) there is direct contact, but not between him and the actor. All the other artists present themselves in their own persons; the actor pretends to be somebody else. However near to his own personality the part he is playing may be, he is always using the words and thinking the thoughts of a being not himself. That is to say, he earns his living by doing something which in ordinary life is considered deceitful and wrong; and the fact that he does it legitimately, openly, and with the consent of all does not make his calling any the less odd.

In ordinary life, as Viola perceived, disguise is a wickedness. Criminals and spies use it to serve their evil or treacherous ends, and in consequence the police and other representatives of law and order may occasionally have to follow suit. Such doings seldom occur in the private citizen's presence and he only half believes in them; and apart from them, he regards a fondness for dressing up as something he left behind him in his nursery. In his secret heart, then, the ordinary man thinks of the actor as a grown person who insists on behaving like a child. This is the barrier which sets the actor apart from his kind far more certainly than any social or professional taboo.

It may plausibly be objected here that every artist is what he is because he carries with him into adult life something of the child. In youth we all have the perception which enabled the child in Hans Andersen's fable to see that the Emperor had no clothes on, and the innocence that enabled him to say so: most of us lose this perception as we grow up, but the artist is privileged to keep it. Consciously or subconsciously, everyone knows this, and it accounts for the fact that very conventional people can never feel at ease in the artist's presence. For the very conventional are people who

have not merely joined in the tacit conspiracy to admire the cut
and colour of the Emperor's new suit, but have grown to believe
in its existence. They are distressed and shocked, therefore, to hear
the artist—tactless child!—proclaiming that the Emperor is naked.

So might run the argument; and the corollary would seem obvious, that the actor's childlike love of dressing up and pretending to be somebody else is all of a piece with the painter's fresh eye
and the musician's uninhibited ear—that he is just one of the artistic family and should not be singled out for discriminatory treatment. Childhood, it might be pointed out, has other attributes
less admirable than honesty of perception; and, in keeping the one,
the artist naturally tends to keep the others also. It is a matter of
fairly general belief, not entirely uncorroborated by evidence, that
artists are apt to be not only childlike but childish, exhibiting on
occasion a sad lack of self-discipline and moral sense. Not content
with pointing out that the Emperor has no clothes on, they tear
off their own and dance shamelessly in the public eye. Could it
be said that the actor, in a family of children so out of hand, was
any worse than the others? Logic might answer no, but popular
opinion would say yes. Whether he deserves it or not, he has the
reputation of being the most badly spoilt of all that spoilt family,
and there are not lacking detractors who doubt whether he has
any legitimate right to belong to the family at all.

It is not the actor's fault if he is a spoilt child. Children do not
spoil themselves. All down the ages society has behaved to the
actor like a most erratic and irresponsible parent, at one moment
loading him with presents and at the next putting him on bread
and water. To be alternately petted and kicked downstairs is an
experience very damaging to the self-respect; and as the other
artists have not had to suffer the same treatment the actor has
always had a just grievance against society. Yet there is something
to be said for society after all; for alone among the artists the actor
uses himself as his means of expression, and the result is that nobody—not even the actor himself—can tell how much of his art
is the real thing and how much is exhibitionism, or to use his own
word, showmanship.

In the other arts, showmanship *can* masquerade successfully as
the real thing, but only with difficulty and only for a time. A painter
may paint a showy picture, an author write a showy novel, a
musician compose a showy symphony, and win an undeserved reputation as an artist; but in each case the work must stand or fall by

its own merit, can be re-examined and dispassionately judged, and eventually finds its level.

This is not true of the actor, in anything like the same degree. Because he uses his own body as his artistic medium, his art is the most elusive, the least simple, the most imperfect, and the least lasting of all. For the same reason, however, it is the most immediately moving; and so an actor with little artistry in him may be able to win and keep a name even among the best of contemporary judges and be passed into history by them, still wearing laurels that he has not deserved. How often this has happened we have no means of knowing, but that it has happened and will happen again we may be perfectly sure. And just because an actor's achievements perish with him and cannot be re-assessed by a dispassionate posterity, there lingers in men's minds a suspicion that the well-graced and much-beloved actor who moves them to tears may be in some way not immediately discernible a trickster, a charlatan. Dr Johnson's famous Club admitted to its ranks all the best practitioners of the arts; but when the name of Garrick, Johnson's oldest friend in London and an actor acknowledged great, was put forward, Johnson felt very doubtful whether 'a player' could with propriety be elected. There can have been no question here of any social snobbery, for Garrick was better-born than Johnson and was received everywhere. Johnson may have been jealous of his ex-pupil's fame; but he had also a genuine doubt whether that fame was deserved.

This uncertainty about the actor's right to be called an artist is not wholly due to the medium in which he works but partly—perhaps indeed chiefly—to the fact that the drama is generally admitted, even by its devotees, not to rank among the 'fine' arts. Every art has its peak to which only the few can climb and breathe the rarefied air, and its lower slopes where the many can enjoy themselves. In the case of the drama the peak is not so high nor the air so thin as in the purer arts; while the lower slopes are crowded with people who neither know nor care anything about art at all. There is something which we are accustomed nowadays to refer to as the art of the theatre, and there is something else which refers to itself as the show business, but just where one begins and the other ends, or just how much one can do without the other, is by no means certain. This uncertainty has even overcome the actor himself, with the result that the more obviously he is only a showman the more loudly he claims to be something better. Down among the conjurors and the acrobats, indeed, nobody refers to himself as anything but an artist—or, more grandly, an artiste.

As to the general playgoing public, it cares not at all what the actor calls himself and, consciously at any rate, reacts much more readily to his personality than to his artistry. The rise of the films, and the public adulation for people whose acting merely consists of appearing in front of a camera and doing what they are told from behind it are sufficient proof of this. Discriminating film-goers know that in the making of a picture only the director has a chance to show himself an artist. It is said that when Dr Czinner, Elisabeth Bergner's husband and director of her pictures, was asked who were the best screen actors, his reply was: 'Dogs and children—but don't tell my wife'; yet comprehensibly enough it is to the well-graced craftsmen in front of the camera, not to the creative artist behind it, that the average film-goer offers his devotion.

So in the living theatre, no audience, however experienced, is fully capable of differentiating between deliberate art and happy accident. Perhaps the best example of the truth of this saying to be found in the history of the English stage is the rivalry between Garrick and Spranger Barry. Posterity, rejecting Dr Johnson's doubts, has had no hesitation in acclaiming Garrick a supreme artist, while Barry is judged to have had not much more than a mediocre talent, enhanced by good looks and a fine figure. The playgoers of eighteenth-century London were a practised audience, deeply interested in acting—so much so that when Barry challenged Garrick's supremacy by playing Romeo against him in 1750, the duel roused the interest of the whole town. Indeed, it monopolized London's two chief stages, Covent Garden and Drury Lane, for so long that an anonymous epigrammatist was moved to protest:

> 'Well, what's to-night?' says angry Ned
> As up from bed he rouses.
> 'Romeo again'—and shakes his head.
> 'A plague on both your houses.'

This much quoted piece of doggerel is significant for my present purpose in two ways. It reflects the intense and informed interest which the ordinary playgoer of Garrick's day felt in the theatre, and shows that in that playgoer's view the contest between the two actors, while tiresome, was not lopsided, nor its result a foregone conclusion. Barry, in fact, was to the eye a more satisfactory

Romeo than Garrick could ever be, and to many playgoers, even the highly trained playgoers of that time, nothing else mattered.

The balance adjusted itself when Barry ventured to play Lear, which was one of Garrick's greatest parts. This time the epigrammatist was moved to very pointed comparative criticism:

'A king, aye, every inch a king',
So Barry doth appear;
But Garrick's quite a different thing—
He's every inch King Lear.

The point here is clearly seen and is very clearly put. Barry can pass for a king on the stage because he looks like one off it. It is an accident of nature for which he can claim no credit, except such as is due to every good professional actor for reaching a high level of technical efficiency. Garrick deserves equal credit for that, and in addition high praise for being that quite different thing, an artist who can imagine his way into the mind of an old, mad king so truly that he can touch responsive imaginations in the audience. Accepting Garrick's superiority as Lear, therefore, let us consider why his manifestly greater artistry could not give him a similar clear-cut victory over the same rival in the part of Romeo. To find this out we must look, not at the two players, but at their audience.

Every theatre audience consists for the most part of people who have come together in search of entertainment rather than of an aesthetic experience; who want, in plain language, to be told a story. They are as ready as children to meet the storyteller half-way, to submit themselves to his spell, to accept his inventions as the truth. But, like children, they also demand to be able to identify themselves with the characters of the story, and are disappointed or critical when the storyteller fails to make any character fit in with their ideas of it. Only a small number of playgoers have the faculty of detachment which enables them at one and the same moment to surrender to the story and to remain conscious that it is a story, so that they can appraise the skill with which it is told.

The more simple-hearted kind of playgoer is quite unable to consider the actor separately from his part, or the part separately from the actor; to him they are indissoluble, a character in the story. This inability is sometimes carried to an absurd length (for example, when Cedric Hardwicke was acting the part of King Magnus in Shaw's *The Apple Cart*, he had a letter from a member of the audience congratulating him on his powers of repartee); but many quite experienced playgoers have it in a modified form. Identifying themselves with the people of the play, they look at Juliet through Romeo's eyes and at Romeo through Juliet's; and if what they see has no strong romantic appeal, they feel disappointed and cheated.

It can hardly be doubted that Barry's Romeo, seen thus through Juliet's eyes, was a much more satisfactory figure of a lover than Garrick's, though it is probable that Garrick's Romeo showed a deeper feeling for poetry and greater knowledge of human nature than Barry's. Nor is it a difficult guess that to the simpler spectators Barry seemed the better actor, while the theatre-wise minority knew that Garrick was incomparably better.

Can we, after this great interval of time, come to any useful conclusion on the point? I believe we can, for the impression left on one's mind by reading contemporary accounts is quite definite; Barry, not Garrick, won the struggle over Romeo, being awarded a victory on points, so to speak. Not merely the simple ordinary public but the skilled and sophisticated judges of acting came to this conclusion, and we can therefore use their verdict to prove two things. One is that neither Barry nor Garrick came anywhere near greatness as Romeo; the other is that a second-rate actor suitably cast may fire the imagination more than a first-rate actor at odds with his part. From this it follows that anybody who sets out to prove that the actor is an artist will have some difficulty in making a clear case if he takes his evidence from any but the highest levels.

If this is true of actors, it is still more true of actresses, for the simple reason that women have always, and inevitably, had stronger temptations than men to go on the stage for reasons other than the possession of dramatic talent. Men at all times have had open to them a number of professions or callings, in almost any of which good looks, personal charm, or physical strength might help them to success. Women, during long periods of history, had only two ways of embarking on public careers—marriage and prostitution. A great lady with a place at court, or alternatively queening it on her own estates, could make her mark in the world; so could a great man's mistress. Other women had to be content to waste talents and personality in private life.

This was the situation in England when Charles II was restored to the throne in 1660. In February of the following year Pepys recorded in a tone of shocked satisfaction that he had for the first time seen women appearing on the stage of London. A new door to public life was open to women; and through that door entered a stream of women whose gifts were as varied as their motives. All these women called themselves actresses, and in a limited sense were so. Whether they could act or not, they appeared in plays. Some of them had real acting talent, some of them acquired a professional facility by sheer practice, some of them had only their physical attractions to display. To make this differentiation was easy enough, but to say with certainty which women belonged to which category was not so easy.

The very first of these women to win a place in history poses the problem. What place has Nell Gwyn in a book about acting? 'Pretty, witty Nell's' morals are not in dispute; they were what is politely called questionable. As an orange girl she distributed her favours as freely, though probably not so cheaply, as her oranges, and when later she moved in higher circles she left nobody in doubt about her standing therein. When her coach was mobbed at Oxford in mistake for that of her unpopular rival, the French Catholic Duchess of Portsmouth, Nelly poked her head out of the window and said jovially: 'Pray, good people, be easy. I am the Protestant whore.'

It is at least arguable, therefore, whether when Nell Gwyn climbed from the pit to the stage her mind was wholly occupied with thoughts of artistic development. Nor did her subsequent career as Drury Lane's leading lady suggest that her hold on the playgoing public was wholly histrionic; there was a fashion for tragedy at that time, and one gets the feeling that some of Nell's impersonations of hapless heroines were tragic in a sense not intended by authors or actress. But in comedy she drew the town, and in the absence of any commentator more theatre-wise than Pepys—a very unreliable critic of drama, with plenty of confidence and no stage sense—we do not know how she drew it. Did she do no more than give her admirers a taste of her own warm, reckless, feckless, and hopelessly indiscreet character, or had she some gift of interpretation as well? If she represented others she was an artist; even if she merely presented herself she must have had stage talent of a kind.

Nearer our own time there is the case of Lily Langtry. Before she went on the stage she was a society beauty whose good looks were so much admired that people stood on their chairs in Hyde Park to gaze at her as she drove by. After a while it occurred to somebody that Mrs Langtry could be admired more conveniently as well as more lucratively in a theatre, and she went on the stage simply to be looked at. At first she hardly took herself seriously as a player and was perfunctory about rehearsals; but after a reproof from Sir Charles Wyndham, who was not the man to tolerate airs and graces, she yielded first to the theatre's discipline and then to its spell, became a tolerable performer, and even went into management. She certainly won the right to call herself a professional actress, but whether she was an artist in any degree whatever remains doubtful.

More recently still the development of cheap printing made it possible for glossy photographs of attractive young women to be sold in the shops for a penny or twopence each, and this fact brought into the theatre a number of such young women, whose faces were their fortunes but whose acting talent was non-existent or negligible. Some of these young women made aristocratic or plutocratic marriages, others had a brief vogue and then vanished into obscurity; but a few remained on the stage, or returned to it later, and became good, professional, reliable actresses. The names of Lily Elsie and the sisters Zena and Phyllis Dare occur to me at once in this connection. Long after the days when their picture postcards had ceased to decorate the mantelpieces of young men who had never seen them except across the footlights, I saw all three of these ladies playing leading parts in 'straight' plays, and can bear witness that all three had become actresses of more than average skill. But how truly any one of them could be called an artist in any but the specialized theatrical sense of the word I should not care to say.

Time marched on, and the films provided a new and vastly more lucrative career for pretty young women who could not act. The theatre began to make greater demands on the competence of its chorus girls; they had to be able to dance a great deal, sing a little, and speak if required. Graduation from chorus to principal became an ambition constantly realized, but it was well understood that girls so promoted were still engaged in the business of entertainment rather than the art of acting. It is not likely, therefore, that the blonde American dancer, Claire Luce, had many visions of turning into a serious actress when she first came to England to play in a tough drama of New York's half-world. Her selection for a serious play, *Of Mice and Men*, was probably no more than an experiment, made because she happened to look the part, and the unexpected emotional power she displayed may well have surprised her as much as it did her audiences.

Robert Atkins saw in her a ready-made Katharina, and a potential Cleopatra. He persuaded her to join his Shakespeare company; and a few years later she played a season at the Shakespeare Memorial Theatre at Stratford-on-Avon as leading lady. She had fairly won for herself a place in the higher ranks of her profession. Examples could be multiplied, but would serve no important purpose. Enough has been said to show how precarious the claim of the actor to be considered an artist can be made to seem. Acting must always be a popular art; and the average audience does not easily discriminate between the various kinds of pleasure which the theatre has to offer, and often turns its back on the imaginative actor in order to exalt the performer who has no asset but his personal charm.

And yet, the old Latin proverb that art is long but life is short comes true once again. Popular performers come and go, and have hardly left the scene before they are forgotten by all but the industrious annalists of the theatre. The names of the artists are not forgotten, but become a living part of history. Why this should be so, and what is the great player's secret, it is my present purpose to inquire. I expect to find that in the course of such an inquiry it will be necessary to consider the nature not only of the great actor himself, but of the audience before which he played.

Chapter 2

The Audience as Collaborator

IMAGINE THAT A LINER MEETS WITH AN ACCIDENT IN THE Southern Seas, and crew and passengers take to the boats. Imagine further that the ship does not sink as expected, but drifts into a coral-island lagoon, and gently grounds herself. Finally, imagine that one man—an artist—is left on board. Probably he was sleeping off a drunken debauch in some remote corner of the ship; you know what these artists are.

Anyhow, there he is, lost on his uninhabited island, but with almost unlimited supplies of food, clothing, and fuel. He can live a life of material civilized ease until he is rescued; or, if he is not rescued, for many years. An ordinary man in this plight could not be expected to last out for long. Deprived of Robinson Crusoe's compulsion to improvise the necessities of life, he would probably drink himself to death from sheer boredom. The artist has resources within himself. Even in solitude he can still find an incentive and a reward in the practice of his art.

If he is a writer, a painter, a sculptor, or a composer, he can work at his books, his pictures, his statues, his musical creations with the hope that some day they may be given to the world in circumstances romantic enough to command attention. If he is an executive musician, more particularly if he is a pianist, he can play his instrument for his own delight, or teach himself to play all the instruments of the ship's band in turn. If he is an actor. . . .

Ah—*there* is the difference. If he is an actor, he is no better off than the ordinary man. He can amuse himself by dressing up, or by grimacing into a mirror; but this will quickly pall, for his desire will be to practise his art, and this he cannot do in solitude. Once again, he is set apart from all other artists by the fact that he is his own artistic medium. Their arts can exist without the immediate presence of an audience; his cannot.

This point, that the player's art does not come into existence until he has an audience, is both simple and fundamental. Yet, like many simple and fundamental truths, it is not widely understood; and until it is understood, there can be no real understanding of acting. Even less widely understood is another simple truth, following logically from the first, that the actor's art is at all times conditioned and limited by the quality of his audience.

Proverbially, the most primitive form of dramatic entertainment came into being when a yokel pulled faces through a horse-collar at another yokel, and the Second Yokel laughed. If the Second Yokel had not laughed, the first one would probably have decided that his performance was not funny, and have gone back into private life. But as it happened the Second Yokel, a responsive fellow within his limited capacity, *did* laugh, and so the way was opened for the eventual emergence of Thespis, Roscius, Molière, Garrick, and Irving.

But suppose the Second Yokel were suddenly to be confronted by Garrick as King Lear or Irving as Louis XI, what then? Is there a doubt that he would find these admired performances meaningless, indeed mad? Garrick or Irving, if they wished to impress the Second Yokel, would have to give him the kind of performance to which he had been educated, and exhibit their highly trained features to him through the horse-collar. No doubt, even so, they would achieve effects far beyond the capacity of the First Yokel, who was by definition an amateur; no doubt they would produce emotional effects in the Second Yokel's bosom to which he was unaccustomed and which he might find upsetting, and would thereby increase his range. But if they tried him too high—if, for example, they introduced the use of gesture or speech before he was ready for these innovations—he would lose interest.

During a tour in South Africa Sybil Thorndike played one of her great tragic parts—I believe it was Medea—before an audience composed in part of negroes. When she launched into one of her big tirades, the natives, who knew no English, were observed to be swaying their bodies in time to the actress's voice. When the tour was over, Dame Sybil's publicity expert quoted this incident with pride, as a proof that even primitive and uncultured Africans needs must love the highest when they hear it. To my mind, it proved nothing of the sort. It proved that there was nothing in Dame Sybil's performance in which the untutored mind could perceive any meaning except its rhythm. All her impassioned interpretation of the thought of Euripides and the language of Gilbert Murray went for nothing so far as these negroes were concerned. To them she was nothing more than a novel form of tom-tom.

In the development of the English theatre you can see this same principle, that an audience must not be tried beyond the limits of its theatrical understanding, always at work. Our theatre, like most other theatres of which we know the history, grew out of religion, and in the earliest plays in our language no attempt was made to invent a story. An audience consisting of people like the Second Yokel and his immediate descendants had not yet reached a point where it could be expected to take in the plot of an unfamiliar story; it could follow the development of one of the Bible stories it already knew, and that was about all. But when the good monks who wrote the early mystery plays got down to their task they found, as later and more knowledgeable dramatists were to find, that characters once introduced on to the stage had to be given something to say and do. The shepherds watching their flocks by night, for example, had to be given time and opportunity to explain themselves, and their audience had to be allowed to get its breath, before the Angel of the Annunciation could be brought on. With the spirit of the Second Yokel still brooding over the scene the playwrights, wise in their generation, gave the shepherds nothing but the crudest horseplay, and the audience—we may be very sure—responded with glee.

Having cut its teeth in this way, the audience was old enough to take in a simple allegory; and the carefully self-explanatory *Everyman* came into being. Later still came that tremendous innovation, the breaking away of the theatre from the church, and the realization that the basic function of a lay stage was not to teach but to entertain.

Even now, the dramatists found themselves strictly limited by their audiences' lack of stage experience. *Gammer Gurton's Needle*, the earliest comedy in English, has a plot so simple that it would serve to-day for nothing more sophisticated than a children's charade, while Nicholas Udall, the headmaster who wrote *Ralph Roister Doister*, lives still in theatre history because he had the sense to put aside his learning and write down to the comprehension of his public. If Holofernes in Shakespeare's *Love's Labour's Lost* is drawn from life, as seems certain, other schoolmasters were not so sensible as Udall.

Shakespeare himself is the first great example of this principle fully at work. Coming as he did at the time of the theatre's swift adolescence and early maturity—remember that the date of *Ralph Roister Doister* was about 1540, of *Love's Labour's Lost* 1591, and of

Hamlet 1602—he had to be extremely careful not to go ahead too fast. Not enough is known of Shakespeare the man for us to guess whether this extreme care was taken consciously or subconsciously. Shakespeare's stagecraft was astonishing and when considered in the light of his own day seems almost impeccable, so the chances are that he knew very well what he was doing when he picked his plots. All we do know for certain is that the plots he chose were the kind that his audience liked, and that the innovations he introduced into them were along the line of that audience's least resistance.

There is no doubt at all that Shakespeare was a supreme storyteller. Why, then, a modern may ask, did he not tell better stories? The short answer to that question is that a man of the theatre must tell the sort of stories that his audience will take. The long-term answer is that it does not matter what sort of stories a supreme storyteller tells, for he will always hold an audience. By way of making that point secure, let us consider in passing one of Shakespeare's least plausible plots, that of *The Merchant of Venice*.

To the modern mind, brought up on realism, trained in the theatre to look upon improbabilities as faults, there could hardly be a worse piece of plot-making than this one. Take its love story, to begin with. Was ever so foolish a stipulation made by a father as this by which a daughter became the predestined victim of the first organized gang of fortune-hunters that came along? Obviously, such a gang had only to put forward three candidates who would each choose one of the caskets, and the girl and her money would be theirs. They could then divide the fortune at their leisure and turn Portia over to anybody who was interested in her.

Her father is obviously a lunatic and yet Portia, though a little troubled at not being allowed to choose her own husband, is very ready to be persuaded that the idea is a good one, and quite determined to abide by it: 'If I live to be as old as Sibylla, I will die as chaste as Diana, unless I be obtained by the manner of my father's will.'

This gives a chance to Bassanio himself, surely a shameless fortune-hunter for the hero of a play, though he is operating on his own and not with a gang. Portia is strongly tempted (in one of her few moments of practical common sense) to tell him which casket to choose, but she refrains. However, he manages, with a little help from the author; and so the whole preposterous scheme is justified.

Then comes Shylock's plot against Antonio's life. The trial scene, and everything that leads up to it, bristles with improbabilities. If the Duke of Venice wants Bellario of Padua to settle the case for him, why does he start the trial without him? By what arts has Portia persuaded Bellario, obviously a professional man of the highest standing, to allow her to dress up as a boy and conduct the case? If she is found out—as in real life she would be, at once—Bellario will be very rightly struck off the rolls. No man of sense, more particularly no lawyer of reputation, would take the risk.

And what fools are Bassanio and Gratiano not to recognize their wives during the trial and to give away their rings after it. In sum, what a carelessly constructed and utterly incredible play. Yet Shakespeare did not run the slightest risk of being told so by the audience for which he wrote. It was an audience for which the whole adventure of listening to stories was still fresh, an audience which had heard few stories, and was eager to hear more and to believe anything. It was ready to believe that all Portia's suitors would abide by the rules. It did not trouble its head about Bassanio, because to marry an heiress and spend her fortune was, in those days, the legitimate ambition of any poor young man of good breeding. It revelled in the trial scene, and had no difficulty in accepting Portia's masquerade as a boy since a boy was in fact playing the part.

Writing for an audience which was not concerned with realism and would not have liked it, Shakespeare took no account of objective plausibility when he wrote *The Merchant of Venice*, but being a supreme storyteller he gave his tale an inner consistency, an imaginative truth, that went beyond mere plausibility, and in so doing he brought off a miracle. His carelessly constructed and incredible play became one of the world's classics.

Even to-day it is the most popular of Shakespeare's plays—the one which is most certain to draw the general public. Experienced playgoers who have seen it too often grow tired of it and become conscious of its absurdities, but before a fresh audience its spell is as potent as ever. Robert Atkins, who has probably as much experience of producing Shakespeare on tour as anybody now living, has told me that in a new town he always leads off with 'The Merchant', and that if other plays in his repertory fail to please the public he always substitutes 'The Merchant', knowing that the public will respond.

In exactly the same way Shakespeare, in writing his tragedies, gave his audience what it wanted and expected. It had a low taste for blood and savagery and a high taste for fine verse. He satisfied both these tastes, and then went on to give his audience something that it did not know it wanted, something to which other writers of his own day hardly aspired—great and true character-drawing.

Here again we must suppose that Shakespeare knew very well what he was doing. He may not have had a thought-out theory that in drawing character more vividly and more in the round than anybody else he was moving along his audience's line of least resistance and was therefore safe. Great artists do not often behave like that, though Bernard Shaw would no doubt like them to. Shakespeare drew his characters more vividly because he saw them more clearly than others; and being a man of the theatre before all else he had the dramatist's special faculty of seeing his work, as he wrote it, through the eyes of his audience, and of feeling what the response to it would be.

As this book is to be about actors and only incidentally about dramatists, it would be an unnecessary digression to trace in more detail the influence that Shakespeare's development of the art of character-drawing must have had upon the theatre-going public of his time. It is enough to point out here that before Shakespeare began writing, the characters in plays were almost as incredible as the plots; while by the time he had done, the characters—*his* characters, at any rate—were so much alive that sometimes they tore the plots to pieces.

For example, Othello is tremendously alive and real, and so is Iago; and in essence the scenes in which Iago undermines Othello's faith in Desdemona are great drama. But because Shakespeare knew that his audience would accept the story without cavil he saved himself stage time and allowed Othello to be convinced of Desdemona's guilt (as we see it) too easily. This is a proof, which could be multiplied many times if necessary, that Shakespeare was wise not to give his audience a kind of plot to which it was not used. Probably if he had spent as much time as we should now think necessary in making the case against Desdemona stronger, his audience would have felt he was labouring the point and would have grown bored and restive.

As regards the technique of storytelling, then, Shakespeare had no incentive to enlarge the experience of his audience. In the matter of character-drawing, however, he had such an incentive, and that remains his great gift to the English theatre. For so far as England is concerned it was because Shakespeare had accustomed his audience to accept—indeed, to expect—lifelike character-drawing that great acting became possible. The first name upon our roll of great actors is that of Richard Burbage, who created most of the great Shakespearean parts as they came from their author's hand. We know little enough about him; so little, indeed, that our belief that he was a great actor is based on a conviction that he must have been rather than on proof that he was. After him the roll of great players becomes a matter of historical record, and every single name that appears on it is that of a man or woman who at one time or another distinguished himself or herself in one of the great Shakespearean parts.

Now it is the quality of Shakespeare that, great tragic poet though he was, he does not lend himself easily to mere rhetoric or rodomontade. An actor launched on one of his famous speeches is under constant temptation to lose or abandon the meaning of the words and to trust only to their poetic beauty to carry him through to triumph. He does so at his peril. The old story of the actor in *Hamlet* who, finding himself unsure of his lines, substituted a passage from *Macbeth* and was received with thunders of applause, carries with it its own criticism. He was a very bad actor to have lulled his audience into a condition so near trance.

An experience of my own sheds some light here. A friend who had a magnificent gramophone invited me to listen to some new records, among which was one of Henry Ainley speaking the 'To be or not to be' soliloquy from *Hamlet*. Ainley's voice was one of the finest organs ever heard on the modern English stage, and as the familiar words rolled out I was suddenly overcome by a sense of quite intolerable beauty and found myself, to my own shame and my friend's triumphant delight, crying my eyes out. Not many months later Ainley played Hamlet at a special performance and I found myself listening dry-eyed and without much pleasure to the same voice speaking the same words in the same cadences.

The reason for the difference in my reactions was only too sadly clear. When the soliloquy was spoken as a separate recitation I had taken its meaning for granted, since I knew the passage practically by heart, and this had left me at the mercy of the music of Ainley's voice. Spoken in its context as part of an analysis of Hamlet's mind and character, the soliloquy had to be understood as well as heard, and by the time Ainley arrived at it he had made it painfully clear that he did not very greatly care what Hamlet was talking about. If his mind was engaged at all, it was set not on the sense but only on the sound of the words he was speaking; and the result was that his Hamlet was one of this actor's few notably bad performances, and was actually overshadowed by the Horatio of Godfrey Tearle.

John Gielgud's Hamlet, which necessarily lacked the strong vocal music of Ainley's, was the outstanding Hamlet of a generation precisely because the actor's mind was on the meaning of every syllable that he uttered, and the verse sounded on his lips as if it had been that moment imagined in his brain and never before spoken. And I take it that Coleridge's famous comment that listening to Edmund Kean was 'like reading Shakespeare by flashes of lightning' places Kean as a kind of cross between Ainley and Gielgud. The flashes came when Kean's mind was on what he was saying; the intervening periods of darkness came when he allowed himself to be carried away by the concord of sweet sounds.

To contemplate Shakespeare's figure from this point of view is to become gradually aware of another complementary figure, more conjectural and less substantial than his but equally necessary to the composition of any picture of the theatre in which he worked—the figure of the Elizabethan audience. By direct evidence we know almost nothing about this audience, though Hamlet in his advice to the players touches on some of its faults and shows that the Second Yokel was among those present. By inference, on the other hand, we can hardly escape the conclusion that it was one of the most rewarding audiences for which a great dramatist, or great group of dramatists, ever had the good fortune to write.

It was too young and fresh—too childlike, in a word—to refuse to meet the playwright on his own ground; he had only to say 'let's pretend' and it was ready to listen. And yet, simple and unsophisticated though this audience certainly was in one way, in others it must have been theatre-wise to a degree which playgoers of the present age must regard with envy.

The proof lies in that astonishing progress in the technique of his art, to which reference has already been made, which Shakespeare made during the comparatively few years of his working life. The progress from *Love's Labour's Lost* to *Hamlet* could only have been made possible in eleven years by the readiness and ability of the audience to develop its own powers at the same rate. Shakespeare —and, of course, the other writers of his day, though to a smaller degree—made huge demands on the powers of his audience, and the popularity of his plays shows that he did not make them in vain.

It may be asked what these demands were, and it may be doubted whether they were in fact so huge. After all, the two great difficulties that confront a modern audience at a Shakespeare production—the fact that his plays are in a forgotten idiom, and mainly in verse—were not difficulties to a generation which spoke the idiom and was used to the verse. Where, then, was the Elizabethan audience required to show such high mettle?

The sufficient and devastating answer is that it was required, for the first time in the history of the English stage, to think, and to think quickly. Shakespeare was a theatre man bred, though not born, and the kind of thinking he expected of his audience was theatrical thinking, mass thinking. He knew from close experience that a dramatist, like a schoolmaster in class, can only move ahead at the pace of the main body of his hearers; that he has to allow the quickest-minded to leap ahead of him, and the slow to struggle behind if they must. And yet, how swift was the pace he felt himself able to set as his powers ripened. How firm was his reliance on his audience when he gave it, not the flat characterization and simple humours which had satisfied it hitherto, but the full portraiture and sophisticated wit of a Falstaff. With what confidence he trusted it to accept his increasing use of the unfamiliar medium of prose. And if his reference in *Romeo and Juliet* to the two-hour traffic of the stage is to be taken literally, how little did he feel any need of slowing down his action to let the laggards catch up.

Every actor and every dramatist knows, often to his cost, the importance in the theatre of the audience's speed of uptake. It is sometimes said that the actor's chief secret is a sense of timing, and that it is because of his superior timing that the professional must always be a better actor than the amateur of equal natural talent. An audience which, in a comedy scene, sees the point of a line at once and laughs quickly is a godsend to a harassed actor, who otherwise must wait to see whether the laugh is coming, and continue his speech before the wait becomes noticeable if no laugh comes at all. If he times this wrongly, and begins to speak again just as the belated laugh comes, his next line is drowned and he has to make up his mind whether to repeat it or let it be lost.

An intelligent audience smooths out such difficulties in the actor's way, and increases enormously the speed and precision of the performance as a whole. But let me here make clear once and for all that by an intelligent audience I do not mean an audience composed of intelligent or educated people; for such an audience can on occasion be very slow indeed. I mean an audience trained to the theatre so that it can follow the dramatist's meaning like a pack of hounds on a scent. Such an audience invariably comes into being whenever the tide of public interest in the stage rises to the flood, and at such periods dramatists can write and actors can play with confidence that their finer strokes will find appreciation.

The Elizabethans were the first Englishmen to have the chance to become an audience of this kind, for it was in their time that the theatre became a profession. Perhaps, then, it was historically certain that at that particular time in our national development, even without Shakespeare, we should have evolved an audience, actors, and dramatists who, driving one another on, would make this opening chapter of our stage's history a great one. Given the questing, eager spirit of the times, perhaps it was certain that the mysterious laws of supply and demand would operate to produce dramatists like Marlowe or Ben Jonson and actors like Burbage or Alleyn.

Great talents usually appear whenever the times are ripe for them, but transcendent genius knows no law but itself. It was the extraordinary good fortune of our theatre that its transcendent genius appeared early in its career, yet not so early that his powers were wasted; that Shakespeare found the Elizabethan audience waiting for him. Because it was ready to follow where he led he was able to give it the plays which, to almost every generation of English-speaking people from his time to ours, have been the accepted test by which the greatest actors have been content to be judged.

If Shakespeare had not been born the other Elizabethans would no doubt have established a fine tradition of acting, and have brought greatness to the stage of their own time. But not one of them, as we now know by a mass of evidence covering three centuries and a half, had that astonishing breadth of human understanding that was to keep Shakespeare's characters alive and fresh when theirs had become quaint relics of the past. Once Shakespeare had written, great acting was not merely possible; it was inevitable at any time when a playgoing public that could appreciate greatness should come along.

Each generation of playgoers since that time has had the theatre it deserved. Sometimes it has deserved great acting, and has had it. Certain names in the long roll of our favourite players stand out from the rest; they belong to the men and women who were acclaimed great by the best judges of their own time. These men and women have known the actor's secret if anybody has; they must have possessed some quality in common that gave them their power. If we bring them before us in procession, like the kings in Macbeth's vision, we shall find out what kind of people they were in themselves, what kind of players they were, and what effect they had upon what sort of playgoers; and so perhaps be able to make a guess at the special quality which made them great.

Chapter 3

BURBAGE AND BETTERTON

BURBAGE, SHADOWY FIGURE THOUGH HE IS, MUST HEAD THE procession. What kind of man he was we do not know but, although we have no detailed account of his acting, there are enough casual references to prove that his contemporaries had no doubt at all of his greatness. Not only Shakespeare, but Ben Jonson, Webster, and Beaumont and Fletcher had leading parts created by him. Several dramatists introduced him into their plays in his own character—sure proof of his hold over the public. There is good evidence that he was the original Lear, the original Othello, the original Hamlet.

Here, however, we are concerned not only with historical facts about Burbage, but also with his methods; and about these there is hardly any direct evidence at all. Scanty references to his appearance show that he was, like so many impressive actors, short in stature. There is a legend that he was not merely short but fat as well, but this does not seem to rest on any good proof.

The only description of his methods which is quoted by the *Dictionary of National Biography* was written by that queer stage-struck Catholic priest, Richard Flecknoe, forty years or so after the actor's death. As Flecknoe was at war with the stage people of his own time, who would not produce his plays, and as the tribute to Burbage occurs in a passage wherein he is comparing these people to their disadvantage with the Elizabethans, we can hardly accept his description as a piece of disinterested evidence. Still there is no reason to suppose that it is not an eye-witness account, belated though it is.

Flecknoe, then, says that Burbage was 'an amiable Proteus, so wholly transforming himself into his part and putting off himself with his cloathes, as he never (not so much as in the Tyring House) assum'd himself again until the Play was done'. Later he adds that Burbage 'had all the parts of an excellent actor (animating his words with speaking and speech with action), his auditors being never more delighted than when he spoke, nor more sorry than when he held his peace; yet even then he was an excellent actor still, never falling in his part when he had done speaking; but with his looks and gesture maintaining it still unto the heighth'.

This, at best, is not a very illuminating account of the man who was described by one admirer as 'England's great Roscius' and by another as 'the best tragedian ever play'd'. To say of a man that he had the faculty for throwing himself into his part, spoke well, and was a good listener, is only to set on record that he knew the ordinary ins and outs of his job.

A much better idea than this of what Burbage must have been like on the stage is to be got, by inference, from the writings of a man far more discerning than Father Flecknoe. Hamlet's advice to the players is so often quoted that it has been worn threadbare, but if we read it again for the light it sheds on Burbage, it comes fully to life once more. For Burbage played Hamlet. These lines were written by Shakespeare for Burbage himself to speak; and he spoke them to the First Player, a man who held in Elsinore a position not very unlike the position of Burbage in Elizabeth's London.

Let us listen, then, from this new angle, to what the real Burbage says to the sham Burbage:

Speak the speech, I pray you, as I pronounced it to you, trippingly on the tongue.

At once it is clear that the whole passage is going to have an impact subtly different from that to which we have grown accustomed. To modern ears, in its place in the play this scene makes Hamlet appear to be taking too much upon himself. Who is he, to tell professional actors how to do their job? His behaviour may be condescension in a prince, but it is certainly presumption in a layman, and the fact that the advice is sound does not excuse him for offering it to people who do not need it. Some modern directors make the players receive Hamlet's exhortations with a kind of respectful impatience; and the First Player, who speaks only to agree with what is being said, is then allowed to make it clear by his intonation that he secretly resents being instructed by an amateur. But with Burbage in the part none of this by-play was necessary or indeed admissible. The audience knew perfectly well that it was listening to the best actor of the day giving a set dissertation on the practice of his art, and certainly did not spare a thought for the incongruity of highly technical instructions coming from the lips of a Prince of Denmark.

To us, then, putting ourselves imaginatively in the place of the

RICHARD BURBAGE (1567?–1619)
from the portrait in the Picture Gallery of Dulwich College

M.ʳ BETTERTON.

THOMAS BETTERTON (1635?–1710)
from the portrait by Sir Godfrey Kneller

Elizabethan audience, one thing becomes instantly obvious. If the scene was written as a *bravura* passage for Burbage, Shakespeare's obvious aim was to arrange that Burbage should be able to provide an object lesson in his own person. The virtues praised by Hamlet must be part of Burbage's make-up; the vices denounced by Hamlet must be those from which Burbage was particularly free, or the whole speech would defeat its own end. It would be the height of folly to make an actor say, 'Speak the speech, I pray you, *as I pronounced it to you*, trippingly on the tongue', unless his own enunciation were beyond reproach.

Hamlet goes on:

But if you mouth it, as many of your players do, I had as lief the town-crier spoke my lines. Nor do not saw the air too much with your hand, thus; but use all gently: for in the very torrent, tempest, and, as I may say, the whirlwind of passion, you must acquire and beget a temperance, that may give it a smoothness.

Now a clear picture of Burbage's acting methods is beginning to take shape in our minds. He can unleash a torrent of passion, and yet hold something in reserve. He can seem to be carried away by a tempest of emotion, and yet be in fact disciplined and in control. And we may be pretty certain that the illustrative gesture which he gave at the words 'do not saw the air too much with your hand, thus' was a contemptuous caricature of one of his less controlled rivals, and got a laugh from playgoers to whom it was instantly recognizable.

A picture in more detail of this kind of actor follows:

O! it offends me to the soul to hear a robustious periwig-pated fellow tear a passion to tatters, to very rags, to split the ears of the groundlings, who, for the most part, are capable of nothing but inexplicable dumb shows and noise: I would have such a fellow whipped for o'erdoing Termagant; it out-herods Herod: pray you, avoid it.

So far, Burbage's task has been easy, for a good actor can always give an effective parody of a bad one. Now, however, he comes to a more difficult task, when he must at one and the same time define the qualities of a good actor and exhibit them in his own person:

Be not too tame neither, but let your own discretion be your tutor: suit the action to the word, the word to the action; with this special observance, that you o'erstep not the modesty of nature: for anything so overdone is from the purpose of playing, whose end, both at the first, and now, was and is, to hold,

B

as 'twere, the mirror up to nature; to show virtue her own feature, scorn her own image, and the very age and body of the time his form and pressure.

It is the liveliest possible description of an easy, natural, and above all intelligent acting method, and it shows that Shakespeare and Burbage knew, as clearly as an actor like John Gielgud knows to-day, that the man who plays Hamlet must never let his mind stray from the meaning, nor try to make up in sound what he lacks in sense, as (alas) Henry Ainley did in this part. Playing of this kind is too subtle for the Second Yokel to appreciate. It is addressed to those better elements of the audience, whom Shakespeare and his leading actor knew they could trust:

Now, this overdone, or come tardy off, though it make the unskilful laugh, cannot but make the judicious grieve; the censure of the which one must in your allowance o'erweigh a whole theatre of others.

The picture is almost complete now; but we may allow the sham Burbage, the First Player, to add to it a few telling strokes, if we think back to the scene in which he recites the tale of Priam's death. In modern productions of *Hamlet* it is customary to make the First Player use a deliberately old-fashioned ranting method. This is particularly necessary—and particularly effective—when the part of Hamlet himself is being acted by a man like Gielgud, who makes his own effects by underplaying. It would not do for the Elizabethan audience, however. That audience would certainly not regard the description of Priam's death and Hecuba's grief as old-fashioned or exaggerated, for it was just the kind of thing to which the playgoers of the time were accustomed. What is more, the first part of the tirade was given to Hamlet himself; and Shakespeare, knowing that Burbage would speak it, forestalled possible criticism from the audience by making Polonius remark how well Hamlet had done it: ' 'Fore God, my lord, well spoken; with good accent and good discretion.'

On this foundation the First Player builds up a performance for which none of his auditors in the play has anything but praise. Polonius is the first to draw attention to his sincerity: 'Look, whether he has not turned his colour and has tears in's eyes.' But Hamlet, soliloquizing a few minutes later, pays him a more detailed compliment:

This player here
But in a fiction, in a dream of passion,
Could force his soul so to his own conceit

That from her working all his visage wann'd,
Tears in his eyes, distraction in's aspect,
A broken voice, and his whole function suiting
With forms to his conceit. And all for nothing!
For Hecuba!
What's Hecuba to him, or he to Hecuba
That he should weep for her? What would he do
Had he the motive and the cue for passion
That I have? He would drown the stage with tears
And cleave the general ear with horrid speech,
Make mad the guilty and appal the free,
Confound the ignorant, and amaze indeed
The very faculties of eyes and ears.

Here, once again, is Burbage speaking in praise of a style of
acting which must have been regarded as the best by himself, by
Shakespeare, and by that part of the public to whom they addressed
themselves with most respect. Here is an actual example of that
controlled passion which Hamlet recommends to the players in
the following act. It is worth mention in passing that the First
Player, for all the wanning of his visage, the distraction in his
aspect, and the tears in his eyes, has himself under perfect control.
Half a minute later he is listening to Hamlet's plans for the play
as though Hecuba had never existed. This, then, is Burbage in
action; a whirlpool of passion and, at the whirlpool's still centre, an
artist quietly in command of himself.

Burbage died in 1619, and though he left behind him many good
actors to carry on the now well-established tradition, no great
player stepped into his place. There were no great new names for
the next quarter-century, and then for a time there were no new
names at all; for the Commonwealth closed the playhouses and
drove the theatre underground. As always when they considered
laws unjust or oppressive, the people of this country found in-
genious ways of evading the ban. Plays were performed privately
at first; later, strange productions, described with considerable
disingenuousness as 'concerts', were presented more openly. The
result was that when London's playhouses opened again with the
restoration of Charles II to the throne in 1660 Davenant and Killi-
grew found no difficulty in getting together companies of quite
experienced actors. But their names were still to make.

The Restoration audience was exactly what might be expected
after ten years of Puritan oppression. A freedom-loving people had
been given back its liberties, and for a time it ran wild, and liberty
degenerated into licence. The Court, fresh from France, exercised

no restraining influence, and the prevailing taste of the time was studied by a succession of clever, salacious dramatists. The London audience became sophisticated; that is, it esteemed cleverness more highly than wisdom, and lost its sense of natural gaiety. Pepys's scornful dismissal of *Twelfth Night* as 'one of the weakest plays that ever I saw on the stage' exactly hits off the attitude; for this enchanting frolic, which later ages have acclaimed as the greatest of Shakespeare's comedies, was so little to the taste of the vitiated Restoration palate that it was hardly ever acted in London from the time of Pepys's last visit in 1669 until 1741. Since then, no theatrical generation has been so silly-clever as to neglect it.

Yet the Restoration audience had great theatrical virtues. It had lost its innocence, but not at the expense of its enthusiasm. It loved the theatre. While the lower orders thronged the playhouses, the intellectuals were busy discussing the laws of drama. Dryden's *Essay on Dramatic Poesie* is the first piece of sustained and deliberate theatrical criticism in the English language. This dialogue between the poet and his friends in a boat on the Thames has the air of being a tidied-up version of an actual debate. We may laugh a little if we like at the solemn talk about Aristotle's unities, for time has shown us that the insistence of the French classical school on the unities of time and place, and the sudden re-discovery of Aristotle as the supreme and final lawgiver, was merely due to scene-shifting difficulties on the new French picture stages. But laugh as we may, we must recognize in this dialogue, which shows some of the best minds in London discussing a subject of deep interest to all of them, clear proof of the existence of a lively and significant theatre.

Dryden tidied up more than his friends' conversation. He tidied up Shakespeare. The loosely articulated plays written for the Elizabethan platform stages could not always be made to conform to scenic requirements in the new Theatre Royal which had been built in Drury Lane in imitation of the best French models. In particular *Antony and Cleopatra*, with its action shifting backwards and forwards across the Mediterranean, seemed to set Aristotle almost wantonly at defiance. Dryden used only one setting for his paraphrase *All For Love*, and wrote a play which held the stage steadily from 1678 to 1790. Since that date none but antiquarians have blown the dust from it, and Shakespeare's original has come steadily and surely back into favour.

It is easy, too easy, to say that the English stage after the Restoration was wholly under the influence of France—that its serious dramatists were imitating rigid French traditions and its comic writers loose French morals. That the French influence was strong is not to be denied; but that it was paramount must not be imagined. Dryden, in the critical essay already quoted, gives to himself a passage of dialogue in praise of English naturalness as against French artificiality. French theory and practice were regarded with respect in London, it is true; but the vitality of the restored English theatre derived from a hearty native quality upon which no foreign influence could have much effect. If it had not been so, there could have been no great work done in that theatre; and it is not to be doubted that the Restoration period, limited though it was in one way and deplorable in another, was one of our great stage periods. Otherwise, Thomas Betterton could not have become—as without doubt he did become—a great actor.

The date and place of Betterton's birth are not certainly known, but when he died in 1710 his age was supposed to be seventy-five, which makes him twenty-five at the Restoration. From the first he was a leading actor, for he played Hamlet at Lincoln's Inn Fields in 1661; and he held his place for an astonishing length of time, for in 1707, when he was seventy-two, he appeared both as Macbeth and as Othello at the Haymarket; and indeed, he died in harness.

If we have too little direct evidence to tell us what Burbage's acting was like, Betterton's case takes us to the opposite extreme. The evidence we have is too direct, too personal, and too detailed for us to be able to accept it as it stands. In the year 1690 a young actor called Colley Cibber joined Betterton's company; and forty-nine years later, having in the meantime established himself as a leading player, a respectable dramatist, and (most surprisingly) poet laureate, he wrote his autobiography, *Apology for the Life of Mr. Colley Cibber, Comedian.* Having strong views, backed by long experience, on the art and practice of acting, Cibber sets them forth; and he exemplifies most of them in a detailed and discursive penportrait of Betterton, with whom he had worked for something like twenty years.

A full description of a great actor by a younger actor of less but still considerable stature, who admired him whole-heartedly and had the gift to put his admiration into words, is evidence of the highest value. But it is evidence that must be used with care, for it is evidence that can hardly be detached and is not likely to be disinterested. Cibber did not draw this pen-portrait of a celebrity merely for the benefit of posterity. He had also an axe to grind. So, while we can accept his purely descriptive passages at their face value, we are at liberty—indeed, we are bound—to scrutinize with care and some scepticism everything else, for it may well turn out to be nothing more than a piece of special pleading, honest but mistaken.

Cibber begins his tribute to Betterton with a passage of panegyric, which gives no picture of the actor but is worth quoting because it establishes the fact that it was in the great Shakespearean parts that he was seen at his highest pitch:

Betterton was an actor, as Shakespeare was an author, both without competitors, formed for the mutual assistance and illustration of each other's genius. How Shakespeare wrote, all men who have a taste for nature may read and know—but with what higher rapture would he still be read, could they conceive how Betterton played him. Then might they know, the one was born alone to speak what the other only knew to write. . . . Could how Betterton spoke be as easily known as what he spoke, then might you see the Muse of Shakespeare in her triumph, with all her beauties in their best array, rising into real life and charming her beholders.

After this, realizing no doubt that general praises, however deeply felt and finely phrased, carry no deep conviction, Cibber gives a particular instance. This is perhaps the most illuminating piece of critical writing that Cibber achieved, as it is certainly one of the most human. The mixture of eighteenth-century literary pomposity with his own natural love of chatter, and the introduction of Addison's sardonic comment on a bad actor, give it life and charm, and the confidence of an expert eye-witness giving evidence on his own subject makes it authoritative:

You have seen a Hamlet perhaps, who, on the first appearance of his father's spirit, has thrown himself into all the straining vociferation requisite to express rage and fury, and the house has thundered with applause: though the misguided actor was all the while (as Shakespeare terms it) tearing a passion into rags. I am the more bold to offer you this particular instance because the late Mr Addison, while I sat by him to see this scene acted, made the same observation, asking me with some surprise if I thought Hamlet should be in so violent a passion with the ghost, which, though it might have astonished, it had not provoked him. For you may observe that in this beautiful speech the passion never rises beyond an almost breathless astonishment, or an impatience, limited by filial reverence, to enquire into the suspected wrongs that may have raised him from his peaceful tomb, and a desire to know what a spirit so seemingly distressed might wish or enjoin a sorrowful son to execute towards his future quiet in the grave.

This was the light into which Betterton threw this scene; which he opened with a pause of mute amazement. Then rising slowly, to a solemn, trembling voice, he made the ghost equally terrible to the spectator as to himself, and in the descriptive part of the natural emotions which the ghastly vision gave him, the boldness of his expostulation was still governed by decency, manly, but not braving; his voice never rising into that seeming outrage, or wild defiance of what he naturally revered. But alas! to preserve this medium between mouthing and meaning too little to keep the attention more pleasingly awake by a tempered spirit than by mere vehemence of voice is of all the master-strokes of an actor the most difficult to reach. In this none yet have equalled Betterton.

And again:

A further excellence in Betterton was that he could vary his spirit to the different characters he acted. Those wild impatient starts, that fierce and flashing fire which he threw into Hotspur never came from the unruffled temper of his Brutus (for I have more than once seen a Brutus as warm as Hotspur). . . . Not but, in some part of this scene where he reproaches Cassius, his temper is not under this suppression, but opens into the warmth which becomes a man of virtue; yet this is that hasty spark of anger which Brutus himself endeavours to excuse.

These two passages certainly fill in the bare outline of Betterton's portrait, but do they make the picture live? Cibber himself obviously feels they do not, for after turning aside for a long and detailed account of Betterton's success in a particular part (which leads him to some very doubtful general conclusions) he ends with an open confession that the actor's secret and the man's genius have eluded him:

I have shown you so many necessary qualifications not one of which can be spared in true theatrical elocution and have at the same time proved that with the assistance of them all united the whole may still come forth defective; what talents shall we say will infallibly form an actor? This, I confess, is one of nature's secrets, too deep for me to dive into; let us content ourselves therefore with affirming that genius, which nature only gives, only can complete him. This genius then was so strong in Betterton that it shone out in every speech and motion of him. Yet voice and person are such necessary supports to it that by the multitude they have been preferred to genius itself, or at least often mistaken for it. Betterton had a voice of that kind which gave more spirit to terror than to the softer passions; of more strength than melody. The rage and jealousy of Othello became him better than the sighs and tenderness of Castalio; for though in Castalio he only excelled others, in Othello he excelled himself.

He ends, almost on a note of anti-climax, with an enumeration of Betterton's physical points. It is not an impressive catalogue, and it conceals under a dull polysyllabic phrase what was probably the actor's most striking feature—his eyes:

The person of this excellent actor was suitable to his voice, more manly than sweet, not exceeding the middle stature, inclining to the corpulent; of a serious and penetrating aspect; his limbs nearer the athletic than the delicate proportion; yet however formed, there arose from the harmony of the whole a commanding mien of majesty.

So much for those parts of Cibber's writing which can be accepted as evidence without question. Now for the passages which I set aside because they related more to Cibber's argument than to Betterton's methods. It will not be necessary to set down these passages in full, but the argument must be completely stated because Cibber comes into direct conflict with the conclusion (which presented itself earlier in this chapter) that one of the marks of a great actor is an ability to speak even the most familiar and hackneyed lines with so exact a sense of their meaning that they regain their freshness, and seem, indeed, to be new-minted in the actor's brain as he speaks them.

I do myself believe that an actor, to be great, must not only be comprehensible but interpretative, and it is therefore necessary to my purpose that an opinion to the contrary so authoritative as Cibber's must be confuted. Here, then, is the particular instance which he quotes. Late in life Betterton appeared as Alexander the Great in Nathaniel Lee's tragedy of that name. Cibber quotes sundry extracts from this work, with a contemptuous commentary on the author's mixed metaphors and forcible-feeble style. He then goes on:

When these flowing numbers came from the mouth of a Betterton, the multitude no more desired sense to them than our musical connoisseurs think it essential in the celebrated airs of an Italian opera. Does not this prove that there is very near as much enchantment in the well-governed voice of an actor as in the sweet pipe of an eunuch?

Having thus stated his theory, Cibber follows up with a more detailed exposition:

When this favourite play I am speaking of, from its being too frequently acted, was worn out, and came to be deserted by the town, upon the sudden death of Monfort who had played Alexander with success, for several years, the part was given to Betterton, which, under this great disadvantage of the satiety it had given, he immediately revived with so new a lustre that for three days together it filled the house; and had his then declining strength been equal to the fatigue the action gave him it probably might have doubled its success—an uncommon instance of the power and intrinsic merit of an actor. This I mention, not only to prove what irresistible pleasure may arise from a judicious elocution, with scarce sense to assist it; but to show you, too, that though Betterton never wanted fire and force when his character demanded it; yet where it was not demanded he never prostituted his power to the low ambition of a false applause. And further, that when, from a too advanced age, he resigned that toilsome part of Alexander, the play for many years after never was able to impose upon the public; and I look upon his so particularly supporting the false fire and extravagances of that character, to be a more surprising proof of his skill, than his being eminent in those of Shakespeare; because there, truth and nature coming to his assistance, he had not the same difficulties to combat, and consequently we must be less amazed at his success where we are more able to account for it.

In Cibber's mind, you see, is a belief amounting almost to an obsession that an actor with a well-trained voice can get all the effect that is necessary or indeed possible by playing a tune on it as a musician does on a fiddle. In this belief, he is shamelessly (but I believe unconsciously) twisting the facts about Betterton's *tour de force* as Alexander. For the despised passages he quotes from Lee's play, though they are over-written and wild, are not devoid of meaning as Cibber pretends. They can be understood. And the play itself is not the turgid nonsense which we are led to think if we take Cibber for our guide. Under its original title of *The Rival Queens* it had earned the admiration of Dryden, an infinitely more perceptive judge; and it continued to hold the stage long after Cibber's attempt to thrust it into limbo. Its headlong passion and genuine poetic feeling made it a test piece for tragic actors and actresses. It seems to me, therefore, that we can dismiss Cibber's attempt to explain Betterton's success in the part, and substitute a simpler and more sensible theory.

If others failed as Alexander where Betterton succeeded, it was because they allowed Lee's whirling words to carry them away into meaningless ranting. If Betterton succeeded where they failed, it was because he alone among them had the great actor's power of control, so that even in the extreme of passion he could make his meaning clear. Without this faculty, he could not have been the great Shakespearean actor of his time; and indeed, Cibber's own description, quoted above, of Betterton's playing in the ghost scene in *Hamlet* lays stress on this very quality.

But why should Cibber have needed to twist the facts, and in so doing to contradict himself? A clear answer to this question emerges as soon as we examine the circumstances. In 1740, when Cibber's 'Apology' was published, the accepted style of acting was stiff, correct, declamatory, artificial, and lifeless, and Cibber him-self was one of its chief exponents. Believing as he whole-heartedly did both that his methods were right and that Betterton was the greatest actor he had seen, he was in a dilemma from which only casuistry could release him.

That he believed his own argument we need not doubt. Yet to my ear there is an undercurrent of uneasiness in his assertion of his views, as if he knew that their validity was beginning to be questioned. 'Does not this prove', he asks in a passage already quoted, 'that there is very near as much enchantment in the well-governed voice of an actor as in the sweet pipe of an eunuch?' That he put this sentence in the form of a question rather than a statement implies the existence of sceptics to whom proof was necessary, and even suggests a fear that the number of those sceptics was growing. I need not press this conjecture too far. It is a matter of history that two years after the appearance of Cibber's book there was a revulsion in public taste which put Cibber and his methods—the 'old style of acting', as it came to be called—out of popular favour. It is not surprising, then, if he had already be-gun to feel at odds with his public, and on the defensive. In several passages we can recognize, if we care to, this sense that all was not entirely well with his theatre; and this is shown most clearly by the tone of lofty contempt which he adopts when he writes of his audiences.

To that point I shall return in a few moments; but first it is necessary to assess at its true value the picture of Betterton which emerges when Cibber's varnish has been removed. Betterton must have been at the peak of his power at the age of forty or so; Cibber did not join his company till he was fifty-five. At that age an artist's skill is at its best, but his physical energy has inevitably begun to decline; the actor, once again, is put at a disadvantage compared with other artists because he is his own medium of expression.

Therefore, while we need not doubt that Cibber saw enough to give him a just idea of Betterton's quality, he did not see the great actor in that inspiring phase of a player's career when he is estab-lishing himself at the head of his profession. Betterton was estab-lished before Cibber was born, and by the time of Cibber's arrival on the stage he had been uncrowned king of his little world for many years. He was a living legend, and he had no immediate successor. Cibber was an experienced actor rather than a percep-tive artist, and what I have already quoted from his book shows

that it was to Betterton's technical ability rather than to Betterton's artistry that he paid tribute. Here is yet another passage in
which this point is made clearer still:

The voice of a singer is not more strictly tied to time and tune than that of an
actor in theatrical elocution. The least syllable too long or too slightly dwelt
upon in a period depreciates it to nothing; which very syllable, if rightly touched,
shall, like the heightening stroke of light from a master's pencil give life and
spirit to the whole. I never heard a line in tragedy come from Betterton, wherein
my judgement, my ear and my imagination were not fully satisfied; which since
his time I cannot equally say of any one actor whatsoever.

This is the highest praise that Cibber, in the cold rhetorical age
of which he was a leading representative, knew how to utter. His
judgement, his ear, and his imagination are satisfied; there is no
more to say. And yet, saying this and no more, surely he must have
missed the whole point of what Betterton meant to his public. For
the stage, and the tragic stage in particular, has for its highest
purpose the satisfaction not of the intellect but of the emotions;
and of the emotions the sophisticated Mr Cibber seemed never to
have heard.

The truth was, because it must have been, that Betterton was
above all a great emotional actor. He knew the actor's secret and
by its virtue he moved men to tears with performances of disciplined power. But the secret is incommunicable, and none of his
younger contemporaries had it. Some of them imitated his power,
and were called ranters; others imitated his discipline, and it is of
this body of followers, who had persuaded themselves that they
were in the true Betterton tradition, that Cibber writes so defen-
sively.

That is the explanation of the Betterton chapter of Cibber's
'Apology'. It was indeed a defence, an apology, not only for his
life but for his style of acting. He knew well enough that the stage
had lost grip of its audience since Betterton's day. Whether he
knew it by instinct, or whether the practical proof of a falling-off
in box-office receipts had brought it home to him, I have no means
of knowing. The point is not material, however, because we have
Cibber's own word for it that the decline was there. And, since
he was not prepared to blame himself or his fellow-actors for the
'corruption' of the stage, he blamed the public.

In a good theatrical period—as I hope I made clear in my sketch
of the Elizabethan stage—actors and dramatists on the one side,
and audiences on the other, encourage one another to try higher

and yet higher flights; and in the end, greatness is both achieved and appreciated. That Shakespeare wrote, and knew that he was writing, for a receptive and rewarding audience is to me axiomatic and needs no proof.

But even an accepted truth can do with corroboration, and therefore let me remind you of the confident way in which Shakespeare appealed to the imagination of his audience in those passages in which, more than in any others, he spoke to it directly through the lips of Chorus in *Henry V*.

> But pardon, gentles all,
> The flat unraiséd spirits that have dared
> On this unworthy scaffold to bring forth
> So great an object: can this cockpit hold
> The vasty fields of France? or may we cram
> Within this wooden O the very casques
> That did affright the air at Agincourt?
> O, pardon! since a crooked figure may
> Attest in little place a million;
> And let us, ciphers to this great accompt,
> On your imaginary forces work. . . .
> Piece out our imperfections with your thoughts:
> Into a thousand parts divide one man;
> And make imaginary puissance;
> Think, when we talk of horses, that you see them
> Printing their proud hoofs i' the receiving earth;
> For 'tis your thoughts that now must deck our kings.

This is no spur to sluggish wits, but an appeal to quick ones. Shakespeare wrote for a stage which knew nothing of settings and little enough of properties, but he knew himself at no disadvantage for that. He supplied his own scenery:

> O, do but think
> You stand upon the rivage, and behold
> A city on the inconstant billows dancing;
> For so appears this fleet majestical,
> Holding due course to Harfleur. Follow, follow;
> Grapple your minds to sternage of this navy,
> And leave your England as dead midnight still,
> Guarded with grandsires, babies and old women. . . .
> Work, work your thoughts, and therein see a siege;
> Behold the ordnance on their carriages
> With fatal mouths gaping on girded Harfleur.
>   . . . Still be kind
> And eke out our performance with your mind.

How flat such an appeal would fall if it were addressed to the wrong ears. And yet how utterly certain of his response was the man who wrote those lines. 'Follow, follow,' he called, with no misgiving at all that his hearers would fail to make the effort, or find it beyond them.

There is no echo of such a feeling when Cibber writes of his public; and that is a sure sign of a bad theatrical period. At such a time, actors and dramatists lose confidence in their audiences and their own certainty of touch. Each helps the other downwards in a vicious spiral, and when the bottom is reached the art of the theatre has ceased for the moment to exist, and only show business and the technical stage tricks are left to entertain a disillusioned public.

Such a vicious spiral must have begun when Betterton passed his prime and nobody of like quality took his place. And Cibber's failure to understand his master can only be understood if we realize that he was writing at a standpoint on the lowest curve of the spiral.

His contempt for the audiences before whom he had himself performed for so long is profoundly revealing. Here is one passage:

Had it been practicable to have tied down the clattering hands of all the ill judges who were commonly the majority of an audience, at what amazing perfection might the English theatre have arrived, with so just an actor as Betterton at the head of it. If what was truth only could have been applauded, how many noisy actors had shook their plumes with shame, who, from the injudicious approbation of the multitude have bawled and strutted into the place of merit?

And here is another, plainer still:

It is not to the actor therefore but to the vitiated and low taste of the spectator that the corruptions of the stage (of what kind soever) have been owing. If the public, by whom they must live, had spirit enough to discountenance and declare against all the trash and fopperies they have been so frequently fond of, both the actors and the authors to the best of their power must naturally have served their daily table with sound and wholesome diet.

Yes, there is good reason for thinking that Cibber was on the defensive; and two years after his book came out it was made clear that his fortress had been indefensible after all.

Chapter 4

GARRICK THE MAN

ON THE 31 JANUARY 1739, CIBBER APPEARED AT DRURY LANE
as Richard III. This was one of his favourite parts, and it came
largely from his own pen, for in rescuing Shakespeare's play from
oblivion he had not scrupled to add to it improvements of his own
—improvements, it must be confessed, so stagily effective that they
were not discarded for a hundred and twenty years. He had been
playing the part, off and on, for thirty-nine years; so his performance must have had some merits. We may imagine, too, that it
gave him satisfaction, for Cibber always had a good conceit of
himself. Only a year after his book came out, however, that performance suffered a cruel eclipse; for on 19 October 1741, at a
little known and newly opened theatre in Goodman's Fields, the
same part was acted in a style as different as possible from Mr
Cibber's by an anonymous young gentleman of twenty-five who
was billed as having never appeared before on any stage; and the
whole town thronged to see it. Soon the word went round that
the new actor was a Mr David Garrick, hitherto engaged in the
wine trade, who had resolved to make the stage his profession. The
old-style actors, conscious, as James Quin their leader put it, that
if the young man's methods were right theirs were all wrong,
resentfully denied that his performance had merit, and hopefully
prophesied that his vogue would not last. But the public recognized
in Garrick's 'natural' acting something for which it had unconsciously been waiting. By May of 1742 Garrick was himself acting
Richard at Drury Lane, and the English stage and public were
swinging in an upward spiral to another great theatrical period.

With the arrival of Garrick, this procession of great players must
come to a pause. This figure must not simply pass across the stage
as his two predecessors have done, for we have too much to learn,
and it is from him that we can hope to learn it better than we
could from anybody else. In my first chapter I compared this book
with a voyage of discovery, but now is the time to add that it is the
discovery, not the voyage, that is important. The ocean we are

sailing has long ago been charted. We are in the position not of the explorer who wants to sail on till he reaches new polar seas, but of the scientists who go with him to examine the ocean bed. Where we find the richest yield of specimens we are well content to drop anchor for a space.

It is not simply because Garrick is accepted almost everywhere as the greatest of English actors that we hope to learn most from him. He is also the actor of whom, as a person, we can know most. At the time when he lived London, though a very large city for those days, was still of a manageable size. At a rough estimate based on the census of 1801, it must have contained about three-quarters of a million people; that is, it was considerably bigger than Edinburgh is to-day, but not so large as Glasgow, Birmingham, or Liverpool. It is to be observed that in such cities the prominent men in society, politics, the professions, and the arts are apt to meet at the centre and to know one another with some intimacy. And in Garrick's London the difficulties of transport made it necessary for most of them not merely to meet at the centre but to live there. Remember that it was in Garrick's London that Swift made his mock prophecy that Partridge, the astrologer and almanac-maker, would die on a certain date, and London was still compact enough—in 1708—to join in the jest and treat poor Partridge, after the appointed day, as if he no longer existed. In such a London, a man of Garrick's fame could scarcely breathe more quickly than usual without the fact being noted and discussed.

And Garrick gave this parish-pump London plenty of matter for discussion. His was a complex character, and many of the men of his own time viewed its complexities without much sympathy. He had many detractors who, since they could not call his professional pre-eminence in question, seized upon his personal foibles, mannerisms, and minor weaknesses, and gave them such undue emphasis that the idea of Garrick in the minds even of well-informed people is still distorted. I have known so able and careful a critic as James Agate, for instance, quote the opinion of one of these detractors as if it were a reasonable estimate of Garrick's character. The particular accusation to which Agate thus gave a new lease of life was that Garrick was mean; the truth is that though Garrick was careful of his money and given to small economies—a matter of upbringing—he was by nature one of the most generous of men, and proved it over and over again. If only to correct such distortions, then, the facts about Garrick need to be set down here in some detail; only so will his character, and the effect that it had on his eulogists and his detractors alike, be understood.

He was brought up in that most galling kind of poverty, the shabby-genteel kind in which lack of money is made more burdensome by the self-imposed duty of pretending that it does not exist. His father, Peter Garrick, son of a French refugee named de la Garrique (anglicized later to Garric), was an officer in the army without private means or professional prospects. His mother was the daughter of a man of Irish extraction who held a minor post in Lichfield Cathedral. The iniquitous system then prevailing, by which rich men could buy army commissions for children still in the nursery, who thus acquired seniority year by year and were enabled to join their regiments as majors or colonels as soon as their schooldays were over, meant that men like Peter Garrick, had little or no chance of promotion and had to remain subordinate officers throughout their service. What was more, in order to avoid half-pay, which in the lower commissioned ranks meant a pittance on which a family could barely be maintained, these men took over those dull or distasteful assignments which their richer colleagues were anxious to avoid. For some years Captain Garrick's wife and seven children saw nothing of him because he was doing garrison duty for a brother officer in Gibraltar. He returned with his health shattered, and made up his mind that his best course would be to sell his commission; but he died before this plan could be carried out.

All this meant that David Garrick was brought up in the kind of home where the first consideration was the keeping up of an appearance of gentility. Captain Garrick and his wife had 'respectable connections', they moved in a circle of socially irreproachable people in Lichfield, and they were well liked in that circle. Inevitably, the pace—even the placid jog-trot of a cathedral town—was too fast for them and they had to strain to keep up. Their friends gave them a certain amount of unobtrusive help. For example, we are told that young David Garrick, stage-struck from a very early age, was sometimes treated to a theatre-going jaunt to London by one or other of his father's friends. But to Mrs Garrick making ends meet must always have been a major problem—Dr Johnson, who was also a native of Lichfield, described the Garricks as 'a family whose study was to make fourpence do as much as others made fourpence halfpenny do' and it is to that fact, and not to any inherent meanness of disposition, that her son David owed the carefulness about small economies which he never shook off, even when he had become a very rich man and, as Johnson also said, 'gave away more money than any other man in London'.

In our own day, exactly the same mixture of carefulness in small matters and great liberality in large ones has been seen in J. M. Barrie. Barrie, like Garrick, had been brought up in a home where the laying out of fourpence was a matter for grave consideration. Like Garrick, he was royal in his generosity in large ways and seemed to have no sense of the value of money when it was reckoned in thousands of pounds. And like Garrick, he retained to the end of his life the carefulness about pence to which he had been brought up. In the last years of his life, when *The Boy David* was in production, Barrie and Godfrey Tearle, who was playing Saul, turned into a tea-shop after rehearsal. The waitress gave Barrie the bill, which amounted to ninepence, and told him to pay at the desk. He hesitated until she was out of earshot, and then said:

'What do I do about the gir-rl?'

'Put twopence under the plate', Tearle replied.

'But will she find it?'

'Yes, she'll find it all right.'

Barrie put the coins under the plate, paid his bill, and went out into the street. On the point of walking away, he stopped dead.

'I must make sure she finds it', he said.

So he and Tearle stood outside the shop gazing anxiously in at the window until they saw the 'gir-rl' clear their table and pocket her twopence.

The stories which are still passed round about Garrick's carefulness, though they are all derogatory in tone, do not in fact reflect on his character any more than this anecdote reflects on Barrie. But Barrie was luckier than Garrick. Although the attitude of the two men towards money was much the same and arose from a similar upbringing, Barrie goes down to posterity as generous, Garrick as mean. The reason is very simple. Garrick was an actor, and Barrie was not. Consequently, Barrie escaped the dislike, amounting in one particular case to venomous hatred and inveterate malice, which Garrick inspired in the theatre people of his day.

The world of the theatre does not change much as the centuries go by, and the standards by which its inhabitants judged one another in the eighteenth century were very much the standards by which they judge one another to-day; and those standards, as I said less precisely in my first chapter, are very much the standards of the nursery.

In the nursery, rules of conduct are not less strict than in the adult world; they are different. Certain virtues—especially the virtue of bearing one's troubles oneself and not going to constituted authority for help—are exalted disproportionately and carried on occasion to lengths that are wrong and foolish. On the other hand, certain attributes or qualities, such as wealth or high birth, which count in one's favour in the adult world, go for little or nothing here. And the unforgivable sin in the nursery is for a child to deny the nursery's code and accept that of the grown-ups. Any infant rash enough to do this is ostracized and tormented by turns, until it confesses its error and reforms its ways.

So in the theatre world, where ordinary values and traditions are notoriously set at nought, there is a special code which can be broken only at the breaker's cost. The first rule of this code is that one of which much literary capital has been made, that the show must go on. Even when all other discipline is flouted, the discipline of rehearsals is accepted absolutely while a play is in preparation; and when it has once been launched, no player worth the name will miss a performance for any cause but serious illness, and some-times not even for that one. But if loyalty to 'the show' is the first theatrical virtue, generosity is unquestionably the second; and this is a virtue which rapidly degenerates into a vice.

All honour to the theatrical professions that, accustomed to vicis-situdes as all must be who depend for their living on public favour and their own individual vitality, they will never refuse a helping hand to a comrade in ill-fortune. Less honour to them that they too easily excuse themselves for taking an easy-come-easy-go attitude towards money, squandering it heedlessly on casual hospitality and undeserving hangers-on. No honour at all to them that they are apt to despise common sense as the sign of a dullard and thrift as the badge of a miser.

The theatre world which Garrick entered professionally in 1741 was exceedingly conscious of itself and very much on its dignity. No longer classed with rogues and vagabonds yet admitted only on sufferance to the company of gentlemen, its members were as strongly imbued with the spirit of the nursery as at any time in history. This is not at all astonishing, for eighteenth-century society had a short way with children or underlings who forgot their places,

and that actors were underlings, and must be kept constantly mind-
ful of the fact, was not seriously doubted in any quarter. In almost
every recorded instance where an actor dared to assert his ordinary
human rights he found public opinion ranged against him.

In Tom Davies's 'Life of Garrick' there are several anecdotes
which remind us sharply of this. The first comes from Paris.
Dufresne, a leading actor, having been interrupted in the middle
of a speech by a gentleman in the pit who told him he was speaking
too low, retorted: 'And you, sir, too loud.'

The audience [says Davies] immediately took fire; the house was in a tumult,
and resented the insolence of the actor who had presumed to talk to a gentleman so rudely. The police interposed, and the next evening Dufresne was com-
manded to acknowledge his fault in very submissive terms. The actor came
forward to make his acknowledgement, and the audience were attentive to
what he was about to say. Dufresne began in this manner: 'Gentlemen, till
now I never felt the meanness of my condition.' This exordium struck the pit
so forcibly that they would not permit him to proceed, but dismissed him with
loud and reiterated plaudits. They reflected, that notwithstanding Dufresne had
rather added to his former affront by what he had said, they did not wish to
make him too sensible of the inferior rank he held in life.

It is significant that in telling this story Davies, who had himself
been an actor in Garrick's company before he had become author
and bookseller, tacitly admits that Dufresne had been presumptuous to defend himself when attacked. He is not so objective in his
account of the extraordinary 'half-price' riots of 1763, when a
certain self-appointed demagogue, a man about town named Fitzpatrick, demanded of Garrick the right to enter Drury Lane for
half-price after the third act of a play. Garrick refused, and the
audience wrecked the auditorium. Next night, presented with the
same demand, Garrick capitulated, but found that the terms had
stiffened. An actor named Moody, who the night before had prevented one of the rioters from setting fire to the building, must
apologize for daring to interfere. Moody, hoping to carry the situation off with a laugh, said he was sorry he had displeased them by
saving their lives; but the audience considered this jest mere insolence, and demanded that the actor should ask their pardon on his
knees. 'I will not, by God,' said Moody, and walked off the stage.

This caused a worse uproar, and Garrick was compelled to
promise that Moody should not appear again while he lay under
the public's displeasure; but in private he warmly approved the
actor's resolute behaviour and told him that his salary would be
paid during his ostracism. Moody, however, seeing that he had

nothing to lose, went to the ringleader and demanded satisfaction. Fitzpatrick, for all his pride of birth, was not man enough to carry off this situation, and consented, after some wriggling, to write to Garrick and promise that he and his friends would consent to Moody's reinstatement.

Even when actors were admitted to friendship by people in good society, on terms of seeming equality, they were constantly made to feel that their presence was permitted only on sufferance. Garrick himself, although for him the barrier really was lowered, had his share of cold-shouldering. We have seen that Dr Johnson, though he had been Garrick's tutor at Lichfield and the two young men had come up to London together to seek their fortune, professed himself doubtful whether 'a player' should be allowed into his famous Club. It is true that Johnson, jealous of his pupil's spectacular success, was apt to say things about him which he would not allow anybody else to say; all the same it is significant that Johnson, with better reason than anybody else in London to know Garrick's unimpeachable antecedents, should be able to put forward such an argument in all seriousness.

Yet even so, Garrick was exceptionally well treated by people of consequence. The 'meanness of his condition' was not often made to stand in his way (though 'Junius' in one of his famous letters did address him as 'vagabond'). He was never made the victim of deliberate cruelty. But in such a world his social respectability would endear him to his fellows no more than a knack of pleasing grown-ups endears a child to other children. Davies hints that Garrick had delayed becoming an actor till after his mother's death to avoid the shock to her feelings that this step would have caused; and the letters written by Garrick to his furious family after he had turned actor are still extant, humbly begging for forgiveness on the strength of his phenomenal success and his feeling that acting was his true vocation. Socially, then, it was a step down for Garrick to become 'a player', and only if he had renounced his respectability gladly, and lived the careless life of what was later to be called Bohemia, would the other inhabitants of his new world have ceased to hold his superior connections against him. He did not. He considered himself still a gentleman, and expected to be treated as such, and in addition he was thrifty. Though he earned high salaries almost from the first, he never flung his money about, and this was something which his stage colleagues could not understand. They thought him merely stingy, and ascribed his larger generosities—when later on they heard of them—to unworthy motives.

Unfortunately for Garrick, his inbred passion for small economies became public property almost at once. As soon as he was
established on the stage he set up an extraordinary three-cornered
ménage with Peg Woffington and Macklin which, however well it
may have worked in other ways, broke down over housekeeping.
The three partners took it in turns to provide, and Peg Woffington,
a lavish Irishwoman, could not bear Garrick's carefulness and
quarrelled with him over the strength of the tea. The incident happened in Dr Johnson's presence, and Boswell recorded it, so that
it is remembered against Garrick to this day; and the theatre
people, while having to accept Garrick's eminence as an actor,
could not consider such a man truly one of themselves.

As time went on, the steadiness of Garrick's private life also set
him apart from the rest. True, a man who shared with a friend
the favours of Mistress Woffington could hardly be said to be
living according to the conventions. The easiness of her virtue was
notorious; and when, after playing Sir Harry Wildair in Farquhar's
The Constant Couple, she boasted that half the audience had taken
her for a man, Quin's retort was that the other half had good reason
to know that she was a woman. But this particular design for living
did not last very long; and some time later the news went round
that Garrick and Peg Woffington were to be married—a situation
which must have surprised the lady as much as it did the town.
Nothing came of this, however, and Garrick's marriage, when it
did come about in 1749, was of a solidity which would have been
remarkable in any age, and in the eighteenth century was almost
miraculous.

There was a certain romance about Mrs Garrick's antecedents.
She was a dancer from Vienna who came to London under the
protection of Lady Burlington and became the rage. Men of
fashion flocked round her, but their enthusiasm was damped when
they found she was not to be had outside wedlock. She and Garrick
are said to have fallen in love at first sight. Whatever the truth
about this may be, there is no doubt of her complete constancy to
Garrick, or of his to her. Davies records that during the whole of
their married life they were never absent from one another for
twenty-four consecutive hours. Confronted with this formidable
example of respectability, it really is not to be wondered at that
the stage people felt that their leader was scarcely of their own
clay. And when his carefulness combined with his steady success

made him wealthy as well, they showed a mixture of envy and resentment. To be rich and respectable was every player's almost unattainable dream, and the less admirable among them could hardly contain their fury that Garrick should be both with comparatively little effort.

Least admirable of all was Samuel Foote. About this extraordinary man's theatrical ability there is much good to be said, but about his character little, and about his disposition nothing at all. He is not the only example in our stage's history of a bad man of high talent being eaten up with malignant jealousy of a good man of talent higher still but he is, surely, the most striking. Davies, obviously struggling not to let his indignation at Foote's treatment of Garrick get the better of him, labours hard to say anything that can be said in Foote's favour; but the sole quality that he can find to praise without reserve is that Foote was 'generous to profusion'. Coming from one actor to another, this tribute need only mean that Foote was just another of those wastrels who made the money fly while they had it, but it does supply a reason why Foote was able to lash himself into a passion on the subject of Garrick's 'meanness'.

Foote elected from the first to consider Garrick his particular rival. How he made this out, even to himself, is not clear. His theatre in the Haymarket was open during the summer season when Drury Lane was mostly closed; and the entertainments which he staged there had hardly anything at all in common with Garrick's productions. Foote was a mimic, a satirist, a mocker at the ways of men and women. His entertainments were a running commentary on the foibles of his age, witty, pointed, and cruel. He was immensely clever and utterly unscrupulous. He 'wantonly ran a tilt at everybody', says Davies, 'and was at the same time caressed and feared, admired and hated, by all'. He did not in any real sense belong to what is now called the 'legitimate' theatre at all, and his hatred of Garrick, if it proceeded from professional rivalry, was merely perverse. The two men inhabited different provinces and each was supreme in his own.

The real reason why Foote, from whom nobody was safe, made Garrick the special target of his spite was, I believe, not professional at all, but personal, and had its roots in the characters of the two men. Foote was by nature a bully, and in Garrick he found what every bully, consciously or subconsciously, is searching for—the perfect victim.

In Garrick's character, mainly admirable, there was one besetting weakness; a morbid dislike, indeed a craven fear, of ridicule. This went far beyond the normal shrinking from adverse criticism, for which actors can very easily be forgiven. Garrick's horror of being laughed at had the irrationality of an obsession, and rather than risk being made to look foolish he would sometimes deliberately play the fool himself. At the time of his marriage in 1749, for example, he actually wrote and put into circulation a lampoon on himself; and again in 1765, on his way back to London after a long absence in France and Italy, he sent ahead from Paris a satirical poem on himself called 'The Sick Monkey', which fell most uncommonly flat in London because in actual fact everybody was anticipating his return with excitement and looking forward to giving him a rousing welcome. A vivid phrase used about him by Arthur Murphy was that 'on the slightest attack he was tremblingly alive all over'. It is a description which calls up the picture of a small boy in a strange, rough school rather than of a grown man who had raised himself by sheer determination to the head of his profession.

And in truth, to read of the relations between Garrick and Foote is to be reminded again and again of every school story in which a shrinking small boy has been tormented by a coarse-grained big one. Garrick was no coward, in the ordinary way. He knew what it was to face and defy an angry eighteenth-century audience, and on occasion—for example, when he decided to restore *Macbeth* to the stage as Shakespeare wrote it, in place of Davenant's then better-known version—how to conquer his own susceptibility to criticism. Murphy's account of this incident attests so much:

Garrick's sensations were quick and irritable, but his resolution was firm and unaltered, as if he said with Benedick: 'Shall quips, and sentences, and paper-bullets of the brain awe a man from the career of his humour?' At length he took the field, confiding in his own powers, and bidding defiance to the malice of his enemies.

Yet before Foote, who not merely knew his weakness (all London knew it) but was ready to exploit it unmercifully, he seemed abject. He sought always to appease, never to oppose.

They met constantly, as was inevitable. They were on terms of apparent friendship, as was perhaps politic. Yet every account of their relationship is consistent with the idea that Foote levied a kind of spiritual blackmail on Garrick, and that Garrick, after every shift and device had been tried in vain, found himself constantly paying up in the form of anxiety and humiliation. Once they met on the doorstep of a house where they had both been asked to dine, and Garrick said: 'Well, is it to be peace or war?' Foote shrugged his shoulders, 'Oh, peace by all means if you like', he said. Is it to be doubted that Garrick's feeling as they entered the house was the relief of the small boy when the bully, in a moment of contemptuous geniality, consents not to twist his arm this time?

The real difficulty in writing of Garrick and Foote is to be fair to Garrick. His conduct throughout was too exemplary. No matter how badly Foote behaved, Garrick bore no malice. If Foote wanted money, Garrick was almost always ready to supply it, on loan or as a gift. They were two of the most sought-after dinner-guests in London, but whenever they found themselves at the same table Garrick allowed Foote to monopolize the talk, and became an eager and responsive listener. Such behaviour in any other connection would not be remarkable, for Garrick was known to be a man of charming manners and benevolent disposition. But it seems almost too good to be true that Garrick's charm and benevolence towards Foote could have been disinterested.

Foote himself was in no doubt on the subject. He thought, and openly said, that every kindness Garrick showed him was part of a campaign of appeasement, and called to him not for gratitude but for an ever-deepening contempt. He took Tate Wilkinson, a young man whose talent for mimicry was fast making London too hot to hold him, into his confidence; and Wilkinson greatly enjoyed seeing Garrick baited, and joined in the game himself as often as he dared.

From Wilkinson's memoirs, written (and very well written, too) long after he had sobered down and had become the manager of the Theatre Royal at York, it appears that Foote hardly ever referred to Garrick except as 'the little hound', and attributed a low or self-seeking motive to everything he did.

Yet the end of the story, which Wilkinson was not in a position to tell, and which he might not have been honest enough to tell in any case, needs to be known. Garrick's kindness outlasted Foote's malice. When Foote's strange, self-centred career as a public success was over, and nobody any longer had reason to fear his caustic tongue, he still found himself helped by 'the little hound'. Even now, it was not in his nature to be grateful, or to believe that the motives of the man he had so hated could be good. Only on his death-bed, in a scene of rather nauseating repentance, did he admit that Garrick had been the best friend he had ever had.

Because Foote was one of the most quoted men of his time, and because Tate Wilkinson's lively but irresponsible memoirs are so coloured by Foote's opinion, a legend not only of Garrick's meanness but also of his trickiness in dealings with his colleagues has been handed down to us and has acquired a certain traditional force. The truth seems to be that Garrick's abnormal sensitiveness to criticism and susceptibility to flattery were always likely to lead him to make a fool of himself, but could never drive him to anything worse.

Arthur Murphy, who was Foote's friend, and who in consequence hardly mentions Foote in his *Life of David Garrick*, gives one concrete instance of Garrick's generosity:

In the outset of life, when his means were slender, he was a strict observer of economy. His enemies gave it the name of avarice. In the course of time, when wealth flowed in upon him in a tide of success, they saw their error but were unwilling to retract it. . . . There are gentlemen now living [in 1801] who, in the hour of need, experienced his liberality. He lent them his money, and, though they afterwards behaved with honour, they must allow that at the time of the transaction their security was rather precarious.

Mr Christie, of Pall Mall . . . had suffered a loss to a very serious extent. . . . It happened that Christie took a ride to Hampton with his friend Albany Wallis, who walked in the garden with Mr Garrick, and told him the particulars of his friend's distress. After dinner, Garrick called Christie into another room. 'And what', he said, 'is this story that I hear from Mr Wallis? If five thousand pounds will extricate you out of your difficulty, come here with Wallis any day you please, and you shall have the money.' This is the account of a living witness, whose grateful remembrance is an honour to his character.

If this story were as well known as certain much less well-documented anecdotes of Garrick's parsimony, Foote's calumnies would have been forgotten long since and we should think of our greatest actor in Goldsmith's phrase, as 'an abridgement of all that is pleasant in man'.

Chapter 5

GARRICK THE ACTOR

FOR REASONS OUTLINED IN THE LAST CHAPTER GARRICK HAS not come down to us an impressive figure off the stage. There were other reasons. His way of speaking in private life was vague, repetitive, and ejaculatory, and his manner was bustling and fussy. It was said in some quarters that this fussiness was deliberately assumed after he went into management, to enable him to keep insistent callers at bay. Certainly in those days theatre managers did need some such defence mechanism, for the relationship between them and prospective authors was altogether different from anything that obtains now. The modern manager who refuses a play sends it back to the author or his agent through the post with politely expressed regrets, and there is an end of the matter. If Garrick refused a play, he was as likely as not confronted with an indignant author demanding to know by what right he had turned the masterpiece down. If the dramatist had influential friends, they too brought pressure to bear, and in some cases actually browbeat the manager into staging a piece which his judgement told him was a very doubtful success, if not a predestined failure.

Dr Paul Hiffernan may serve as an example. He was an exceedingly odd Irishman who came to London about 1754 to make a living by his pen, and conceived himself, with no justification at all, to have a talent for writing plays. A failure at Covent Garden did not disturb his complacency, and he published his next play with a preface complaining bitterly of the unfairness of the managers of both Covent Garden and Drury Lane, who had dared to reject it. The public's judgement supported the managers', yet still Hiffernan felt himself ill-used. His next play was no better than the rest, but Garrick did give it a production at Drury Lane, where it too failed, and was taken off amid the execrations of the author, who said he was being deprived of his 'right' to a benefit, and did everything that he could think of to blacken Garrick's name.

Another such awkward moment in Garrick's life is recorded by

Murphy. A tragedy called *Virginia*, on a theme taken from the third book of Livy, had been written by a clergyman named Edward Crisp, and seems, from Murphy's elaborately careful reference to the plot, to have been an earnestly pedestrian and (from the stage point of view) amateurish piece of work; 'the fable, though it cannot boast of situations to alarm and agitate the heart, is conducted in regular order and a well connected train of events'.

It is hardly likely that a play no better than this would have been staged on its merits, but the Rev. Mr Crisp had a string to pull. He was related to, or had the patronage of, the Earl of Coventry, whose Countess was a reigning beauty of the day. She drove to Garrick's house, sent word that she wanted to see him for a moment on business, and handed him Crisp's manuscript with the words: 'There, Mr Garrick, I put into your hands a play which the best judges tell me will do honour to you and the author.' Not to have produced the play after that would have involved Garrick in major unpleasantness, and we can imagine that he began to read it with a prayer in his heart that it would not prove totally unactable, a point which Lady Coventry's 'best judges' were not likely to be competent to decide. Fortunately, it was passable. Garrick obeyed Lady Coventry 'as if she had been a tenth muse, and prepared the play with the utmost dispatch'.

The tragedy had a moderate success but has never been heard of again; and Murphy makes it very clear, though he does not specifically state, that any credit that was going went to the players:

[Garrick] in the part of Virginius, Mossop in that of Appius, and Mrs Cibber in Virginia, deserved the compliment paid to them by the author in his preface. The representation was attended by another advantage. Mrs Yates . . . made her first appearance on the English stage, in the part of Marcia, and by her extraordinary beauty, and an early promise of great talents, helped to give attraction to the piece. But the great stroke which crowned it with success (which will appear almost incredible) was Garrick's manner of uttering two words.

Claudius, the iniquitous tool of the Decemvir, claims Virginia as a slave born in his house. He pleads his cause before Appius on his tribunal. During that time, Garrick, representing Virginius [Virginia's father], stood on the opposite side of the scene next to the stage door, with his arms folded across his breast, his eyes riveted to the ground, like a mute and lifeless statue. Being told at length that the tyrant is ready to hear him, he continued for some time in the same attitude, his countenance expressing a variety of passions, and the spectators fixed in ardent gaze. By slow degrees he raised his head; he paused; he turned round in the slowest manner, till his eyes fixed on Claudius; he still

remained silent, and after looking eagerly at the impostor, he uttered in a low
tone of voice that spoke the fullness of a broken heart: 'Thou traitor!' The whole
audience was electrified . . . and a thunder of applause testified their delight.

This passage is valuable because it gives us a picture of Garrick
in action which has the quality of a snapshot rather than of a
posed portrait, and gives us at once an idea of what his acting was
like, and an assurance that he could leave the bustling, fussy manner of ordinary life behind him when he stepped on to the stage.
Such an assurance is important, in view of the fact that almost all
contemporary accounts of Garrick's acting agree in laying stress
on the quality of naturalness; and we have now to make up our
minds exactly what this word 'natural' was meant to convey.

We can put out of our minds any idea that Garrick's naturalness
was similar, either in kind or in degree, to the naturalism which
the modern actor has been at such mistaken pains to cultivate.
The statuesque silence after Virginius had been given leave to
speak, the careful working up of the emotions of the audience by
means of facial expression alone, the deliberate heightening of the
tension by the slow raising of the head, the holding of that tension
by a pause, the tightening of the screw in the long-drawn-out
moment till his eyes came to rest on his enemy's face, and the final
breaking of the almost intolerable strain by the utterance of two
words, in themselves utterly banal but now charged with explosive
force—all this would be thought dreadfully theatrical by some
present-day standards. The natural actor of to-day, playing this
scene, would indicate by a slight tightening of the lips his realization that Virginius in such circumstances might feel some pretty
powerful emotions which it was his duty, not only as a Roman
father but also as a British actor, to restrain. He would then say
'Thou traitor!' in a tense, tight-lipped manner designed to show
raging passions within, and the unstirred audience would have no
chance of realizing that a moment had been let slip which a better
actor with a better method had once made great.

Players and playgoers who have been brought up on this negative method of emotional expression are afraid of positive acting,
which they dismiss, whenever they can, with a dangerous general
term of abuse, calling it 'ham' acting. But now there are signs that
the negative period is passing. People are beginning to realize once
again that 'ham' acting is simply good acting badly done. The best
of our leading actors are no longer afraid to go full out for their
effects, and one result of the change is that it has become much

easier than it was twenty years ago to understand certain of Garrick's achievements. For example, it is a matter of historical fact that one of his most successful comic parts was that of Abel Drugger in Ben Jonson's *The Alchemist*. To anybody brought up in the negative, strictly realistic school of acting, this fact seems quite incomprehensible, for the part as written is a small one; and I have heard modern actors and producers, in the years between the two wars, say that they could not imagine how Garrick contrived to make the part worth his while. Now, the mystery is a mystery no longer. Cedric Hardwicke, an actor whose methods were always positive, played the part at Malvern and showed that it had much more in it than had been suspected; and so paved the way for Alec Guinness, one of the leaders of the present-day return to expressive, full-flavoured acting, who filled the part out to ampler proportions still. Given Garrick's power of carrying his meaning without the aid of words, a power much greater than any present-day actor can command, it is now possible to see the part as material for a comic *tour de force*.

We can get some impression of just how great that *tour de force* was from a document only recently made available to English readers, being letters from London written in 1775 as contributions to a magazine published in Leipzig. The author, Georg Christoph Lichtenberg, was a professor at Göttingen, and because he was trying to convey an impression of Garrick's greatness to readers most of whom would never have the chance to see Garrick act, his descriptions of the actor's methods preserve for us details which contemporary English writers took for granted. In his remarks about *The Alchemist*, Lichtenberg is comparing the broadly comic playing of Weston as Abel Drugger with Garrick's much more subtle method:

Ben Jonson has indicated only a few points in Abel Drugger's character; and if a player can once get his line from this, he can proceed more or less *à son aise* with no fear of overstepping the mark. Weston has an excellent opportunity of ridding himself of his own personality, especially in the long intervals when Abel Drugger is dumb and in a room where there are, besides a few astronomers and exorcisers, human skeletons, crocodiles, ostrich eggs and empty vessels, in which the devil himself could sit. I can almost see him, rigid with terror at every violent movement of the astrologer or at the least noise of which the cause is not apparent, standing like a mummy with feet together; only when it is over does life return to his eyes and he looks about him, then turns his head round slowly, and so forth. Most of the audience clap and laugh, and even the critic smiles at the ridiculous fellow.

But when Garrick plays Abel Drugger it is the critic who leads the applause. Here we have a vastly different creature, an epitome of the author's purpose, heightened by a comprehensive knowledge of his characteristic traits, and interpreted so that he may be clearly understood from the top gallery downwards. He does not lack the language of gesture, if I may so express it, in an indolent all-embracing torpidity, which finally, indeed, becomes unnatural; but every moment poor Abel is giving fresh indications of his character; superstition and simplicity. I only mention one feature, which Mr Weston could not even imitate and assuredly could not have invented, and of which I do not suppose the author himself had thought. When the astrologers spell out from the stars the name, Abel Drugger, henceforth to be great, the poor gullible creature says with heartfelt delight: 'That is my name.' Garrick makes him keep his joy to himself, for to blurt it out before everyone would be lacking in decency. So Garrick turns aside, hugging his delight to himself for a few moments, so that he actually gets those red rings round his eyes which often accompany great joy, at least when violently suppressed, and says to himself: 'That is my name.' The effect of this judicious restraint is indescribable, for one did not see him merely as a simpleton being gulled, but as a much more ridiculous creature, with an air of secret triumph, thinking himself the slyest of rogues. Nothing like this can be expected of Weston.

As one reads this perceptive passage one's admiration grows, not merely for the actor whose creative imagination had conceived and whose technical equipment could carry out so subtle an effect, but for the audience which could appreciate and applaud it. It is not to be thought, of course, that there were no members of those audiences who missed the finer points of Garrick's acting; Lichtenberg himself bears witness that 'thousands cannot see all that Garrick has to show them', and that many people thought Weston's Abel Drugger equal or superior to Garrick's. But the mere fact that Garrick put such a delicate finish on his work shows that he could rely on a theatre-wise audience, for no master-cook wastes his most refined flavours on coarse palates. At any rate Lichtenberg is in no doubt on this point, for in another passage he speaks of Garrick winning tremendous applause 'in one of the first playhouses of the world and from an audience of the greatest sensibility'.

It might be thought by some of the more inveterate ham-haters that Garrick's power of expressing a variety of emotions in his countenance has been exaggerated by admiring contemporaries, and might turn out, if objectively examined, to be no such extraordinary matter after all. Against this, fortunately, we have the contemporary evidence of a witness who was unable to be anything but objective. This was a painter called Shireff, who was deaf and dumb from birth. Those were days in which the deaf-

and-dumb alphabet had yet to be invented; nevertheless Shireff had been taught by a 'skilful master in Scotland' not only to read but to write, and write well. Shakespeare was his especial favourite, and when Garrick acted in Shakespeare 'young Shireff was sure to be present, professing that he was the actor whom he best understood'. In 1798, long after Garrick's death, Arthur Murphy was dining one evening with a man named Heriot, proprietor of *The True Briton*. Shireff, who was Mrs Heriot's brother, was present, and Murphy records the scene in his biography:

When the company were seated at table, this writer was told that, if he held up his finger and spelt his words in the air, he might carry on a conversation. He tried the experiment, and found that it answered. Being told that Mr Shireff was acquainted with Garrick, and admired him as an actor, he put the following questions to him: 'Did you know Garrick?'—'Yes,' in a very inarticulate sound.—'Did you ever see him act?'—'Yes.'—'Did you admire him?'—'Yes.' —'How could that be, when you could not hear him, and of course, could not understand him?' The answer was unintelligible. Mr and Mrs Heriot were used to his manner; at their desire, the question was repeated, and the answer, when explained, astonished the whole company. Mr Shireff's reply was, *Garrick's face was a language*. To prove that it was so, Mr Shireff stood up after dinner, and, muttering uncouth sounds, went through the part of 'Richard III' by his deportment, his action, and most significant looks, distinguishing every scene and all the various situations of Richard from the beginning to his death in Bosworth field. Hence a judgement may be formed of the actor, who could play before the deaf and dumb and make them capable. *His face was a language!*

Yet in spite of this unique power of expression, used to the full as it obviously was, still the adjective which comes most easily to the pens of those who set out to describe Garrick's acting was 'natural'. Oliver Goldsmith, for example, playing that eighteenth-century forerunner of the truth game which consisted in writing an epitaph in advance for one of your friends, said:

On the stage he was natural, simple, affecting;
'Twas only that when he was off he was acting.

This corroborates what has been said already, that Garrick shed his mannerisms when he went on the stage, but it leaves us still face to face with the problem: in what sense can an art so elaborately theatrical as Garrick's be truly described as natural, or still more as simple?

The answer to this has been given, in part at any rate, by Henry Fielding, in the chapter of *Tom Jones* in which Tom and Partridge escort Mrs Miller and her youngest daughter to see Garrick play Hamlet at Drury Lane. The passage is very frequently quoted, but

I make no apology for taking it once more out of its context; for its claim to be included in a book whose special study is the effect of great actors upon their audiences is beyond question. The innocent Partridge, out of whose reactions to the play Tom had promised himself in advance so much amusement, cannot be a figure entirely of his author's invention. I do not question that Fielding must have heard some unsophisticated playgoer talk in the same strain, and that this gave him the idea of sending Tom and his party to the play. The scene is inserted in the novel for its own sake, and has no bearing at all on the development of the plot. Here then are the relevant passages:

As soon as the play began, Partridge was all attention, nor did he break silence till the entrance of the ghost: upon which he asked Jones, what man that was in the strange dress: 'Something', said he, 'like what I have seen in a picture. Sure it is not armour, is it?' Jones answered: 'That is the ghost.' To which Partridge replied, with a smile: 'Persuade me to that, sir, if you can. Though I can't say I ever saw a ghost in my life, yet I am certain I should know one, if I saw him, better than that comes to. No, no, sir; ghosts don't appear in such dresses as that, neither.' In this mistake, which caused much laughter in the neighbourhood of Partridge, he was suffered to continue, till the scene between the ghost and Hamlet, when Partridge gave that credit to Mr Garrick which he had denied to Jones, and fell into so violent a trembling that his knees knocked against each other. Jones asked him what was the matter, and whether he was afraid of the warrior upon the stage. 'Oh la! Sir,' said he, 'I perceive now it is what you told me. I am not afraid of anything; for I know it is but a play: and if it was really a ghost, it could do one no harm at such a distance, and in so much company: and yet if I was frightened, I am not the only person.' 'Why, who,' cries Jones, 'dost thou take to be such a coward here besides thyself?'—'Nay, you may call me a coward if you will; but if that little man there upon the stage is not frightened, I never saw any man frightened in my life.'

A little later he returns to the point, excusing himself:

'Not that it was the ghost that surprised me, neither; for I should have known that to be only a man in a strange dress: but when I saw the little man so frightened himself, it was that which took hold of me.' 'And dost thou imagine then, Partridge,' cries Jones, 'that he was really frightened?'—'Nay, sir,' said Partridge, 'did you not yourself observe afterwards, when he found it was his own father's spirit . . . how his fear forsook him by degrees, and he was struck with sorrow, as it were, just as I should have been, had it been my own case?'

So the play still runs its course, with Partridge still swinging backwards and forwards between the two worlds of reality and make-belief. When all is done, Jones asks him which of the players he has liked best:

To this he answered, with some appearance of indignation at the question: 'The

DAVID GARRICK (1717–79)
from the bust at the Garrick Club

AN EIGHTEENTH-CENTURY AUDIENCE
from an engraving after William Hogarth

king, without doubt.'—'Indeed, Mr Partridge,' says Mrs Miller, 'you are not of the same opinion with the town; for they are all agreed, that Hamlet is acted by the best player who was ever on the stage.'—'He the best player!' cries Partridge, with a contemptuous sneer: 'Why, I could act as well as he himself. I am sure, if I had seen a ghost, I should have looked in the very same manner, and done just as he did. And then, to be sure, in the scene, as you called it, between him and his mother, where you told me he acted so fine, why, Lord help me! any man, that is, any good man, that has such a mother, would have done exactly the same. I know you are only joking with me; but, indeed, madam, though I was never at a play in London, yet I have seen acting before in the country; and the king for my money: he speaks all his words distinctly, half as loud again as the other. Anybody may see he is an actor.'

We may take it that the sophisticated Tom, the sensible Mrs Miller, and the artless Partridge made up a very fair cross-section of a Drury Lane audience, and all three in their very different ways attest the truth of Goldsmith's description—'natural, simple, affecting'. Garrick's methods may have been, by the standards of modern audiences, artificial, but his appeal was direct. Besides this, the point must not be overlooked that Garrick's playing seemed more realistic to his contemporaries than it does to us because it *was* more realistic. If Garrick appears to us to exhibit his emotions too freely on the stage, so did the contemporary man in the street. Englishmen had not then set themselves to disguise the fact that they are an emotional race. When Partridge felt fear, he 'fell into so violent a trembling that his knees knocked against each other', and therefore would think it only natural that Hamlet should suffer similar paroxysms.

We can prove, as it happens, how little Fielding exaggerated; for Lichtenberg had read *Tom Jones*, and in his own description of Garrick as Hamlet he covers the same ground as Fielding, not with any desire to substitute fact for fiction, but simply to fill in details which Fielding, limiting himself to Partridge's field of vision, has had to omit. These details are very full, for Lichtenberg had a clear objective eye and a truly German thoroughness:

Suddenly, as Hamlet moves towards the back of the stage slightly to the left and turns his back on the audience, Horatio starts, and saying: 'Look, my lord, it comes,' points to the right, where the ghost has already appeared and stands motionless, before anyone is aware of him. At these words Garrick turns sharply and at the same moment staggers back two or three paces with his knees giving way under him; his hat falls to the ground, and both his arms, especially the left, are stretched out nearly to their full length, with the hands as high as his head, the right arm more bent and the hand lower, and the fingers apart; his mouth is open: thus he stands rooted to the spot, with legs apart, but no loss of

C

dignity, supported by his friends, who are better acquainted with the appari-
tion and fear lest he should collapse.

To a reader without the special theatrical imagination, that description may give an impression of absurdity—the same absurdity
as the figure of an actor on a film would have if the machine were
stopped and he were fixed rigid in an attitude of terror. But the
absurdity passes as Lichtenberg releases Garrick from his attitude
and goes on to describe its effect:

His whole demeanour is so expressive of terror that it made my flesh creep even
before he began to speak. The almost terror-struck silence of the audience, which
preceded this appearance and filled one with a sense of insecurity, probably did
much to enhance this effect. At last he speaks, not at the beginning, but at the
end of a breath, with a trembling voice: 'Angels and ministers of grace, defend
us!' words which supply anything this scene may lack and make it one of the
greatest and most terrible that will ever be played on any stage.

The ghost beckons. Hamlet draws his sword 'with a swiftness that
makes one shudder' on his friends who are holding him back. The
ghost leaves the stage:

Hamlet still remains motionless, his sword held out . . . and at length, when the
spectator can no longer see the ghost, he begins slowly to follow him, now standing still and then going on, with sword still upon guard, eyes fixed on the ghost,
hair disordered, and out of breath, until he too is lost to sight. You can well
imagine what loud applause accompanies this exit. It begins as soon as the
ghost goes off the stage and lasts until Hamlet also disappears. What an amazing
triumph it is.

It is clear from all kinds of contemporary references that the
quality which differentiated Garrick from all other players of his
time was something beyond mere realism. Everybody agrees that
the quality was there, but few have attempted to account for it,
and most of those few have failed. If Davies's powers had been
equal to the occasion his evidence would have been most valuable,
for he, as an ex-actor, might have been expected to have the
craftsman's preoccupation with methods rather than the critic's
concern with effects. Davies, however, makes a very poor and
perfunctory job of his analysis of Garrick's Hamlet.

Murphy does a little better, but comes to his task in a defeatist
mood, beginning with the remark that it is impossible that Garrick, as an actor, should receive the justice due to his merit from
the pen of any writer whatever. 'To form an adequate idea of such
a genius, it is necessary that he should be seen, heard, and felt. . . .
When we have said . . . that he was graceful in his movements,

and that his countenance expressed his inmost feelings, and his elocution was consonant to every passion and sentiment, how far will that description go towards a full and just idea of the performer?'

Conscious that he is not doing very well so far, Murphy now brings forward the excuse that Cibber in his time had had the same difficulty with Betterton, and then, encouraged perhaps by the spectacle of a companion in his distress, produces something a little more illuminating:

Garrick's imagination was so strong and powerful that he transformed himself into the man he represented, and his sensibility was so quick that every sentiment took immediate possession of him. Before he uttered a word, the varying passions began to work, and wrought such rapid changes in his features, in his action, his attitudes, and the expression of his eye, that he was, almost every moment, a new man.

This seems to make of Garrick a sort of human chameleon, rather than a conscious artist, but it gives us something to go on. Murphy then quotes Cibber's passage about Betterton in Hamlet's scene with the ghost,[1] and says at the end of it: 'This is an exact description of Garrick. In this situation, the two great actors seem to vie with one another.' In another respect, however, that of physical equipment, he gives Garrick a complete victory. 'Like Betterton, he did not rise above the middle size, but he was of a delicate frame, his limbs in just proportion; his voice clear and melodious, and his eyes looked the very soul.'

This is good conscientious eulogism, but nothing much more. It lacks warmth, and considering that Murphy was a successful dramatist who worked with Garrick for many years—amicably, except for a sharp struggle over Murphy's tragedy *The Orphan of China*, in which Garrick accepted defeat with a good grace—it lacks the touch of intimate knowledge. It could have been written by any hack obituarist who had never seen Garrick in his life, and I can only feel that Murphy's sense of inadequacy had clogged his pen. Let me therefore add a few sentences by another contemporary writer, whose chief fault was that he never considered himself inadequate to anything.

Richard Cumberland in his *Memoirs* describes how, as a boy of sixteen, he had seen Quin and Garrick acting together as Horatio and Lothario in Rowe's *The Fair Penitent*. He first describes Quin,

[1] See p. 38.

impressive but stiff and stylized in the manner of the old school, and then continues:

But when . . . I first beheld little Garrick, young and light and alive in every muscle and in every feature, heavens, what a transition! It seemed as if a whole century had been stepped over in the transition of a single scene; old things were done away, and a new order at once brought forward, bright and luminous, and clearly destined to dispel the barbarism and bigotry of a tasteless age, too long attached to the prejudices of custom, and superstitiously devoted to the illusions of imposing declamation.

This lightning sketch, an old man's vivid recollection of a great moment in his impressionable youth, gives something of Garrick which must escape the biographer labouring to give a famous man his due appreciation. With a touch like this, the figure of Garrick that we are piecing together begins to take life, and the glow of his genius to give out a warmth that our senses can catch.

Yet there is still lacking some breath of reality. How does this artist Garrick, young and light and alive in every muscle and feature, whose eyes looked the very soul, who could at will be frightened if ever man was frightened, blend with the fussy worka-day Garrick his enemies saw, who ran Drury Lane and saved his money and could not bear criticism and was mean about candles and tea? Neither figure quite comes to life. One seems too much composed of light and air, too divinely inspired for this world; the other has too much of the journeyman in him to be acceptable as a genius. Some further element is necessary if they are to fuse and become one human being.

For myself, I find that element in a quality of Garrick's which most of his contemporaries seem either to have taken for granted or to have underrated; his extraordinary thoroughness in matters of artistic detail, that 'infinite capacity for taking pains', which is the less spectacular side of genius. His gift for the stage was excep-tional, and he was much better fitted physically to be a great actor than most of his rivals; yet it was not because of these strokes of fortune that he outdistanced them, but because he had a more original mind than they had, and was ready to use it to work harder than they did. In an age when the technique of acting had become stereotyped he alone had the courage and the vision to take nature for his model; and in an age when it was taken for granted that Shakespeare's plays could not be acted with effect except in adaptations, he alone had the questing spirit which im-pelled him to read the plays in the original and restore them to the stage where he could. It is true that to our ideas Garrick's restoration of Shakespeare seems as inadequate as his boast that he would 'lose no drop of that immortal man' seems unfulfilled. It is true that he was himself guilty of making far-reaching 'improvements' to the last act of *Romeo and Juliet* without shame or self-reproach, and amid general applause. But the fact remains that before Garrick's advent Shakespeare was a neglected old classic, seldom taken from the shelf; and that from the day of Garrick's first appearance as Richard III few of Shakespeare's major plays have again been allowed to drop out of the stage's repertory.

On the subject of Garrick's thoroughness Murphy, at ease in his narrative stride and not yet stultifying himself in a final assessment of his subject, has a valuable and revealing passage when he describes the actor's handling of the part of King Lear, and more particularly his manner of approach to the mad scenes:

It was in Lear's madness that Garrick's genius was remarkably distinguished. He had no sudden starts, no violent gesticulation; his movements were slow and feeble, misery was depicted in his countenance; he moved his head in the most deliberate manner; his eyes were fixed, or, if they turned to any one near him, he made a pause, and fixed his look on the person after much delay; his features at the same time telling what he was going to say before he uttered a word. During the whole time he presented a sight of woe and misery, and a total alienation of mind from every idea, but that of his unkind daughters.

He was used to tell how he acquired the hints that guided him, when he began to study this great and difficult part. He was acquainted with a worthy man who lived in Leman Street, Goodman's Fields; this friend had an only daughter, about two years old; he stood at his dining-room window, fondling the child and dangling it in his arms, when it was his misfortune to drop the infant into a flagged area, and killed it on the spot. He remained at his window screaming in agonies of grief. The neighbours flocked to the house, took up the child, and delivered it dead to the unhappy father, who wept bitterly, and filled the street with lamentations. He lost his senses, and from that moment never recovered his understanding.

As he had a sufficient fortune, his friends chose to let him remain in his house, under two keepers appointed by Dr Monro. Garrick frequently went to see his distracted friend, who passed the remainder of his life going to the window, and there playing in fancy with his child. After some dalliance, he dropped it, and, bursting into a flood of tears, filled the house with shrieks of grief and bitter anguish. He then sat down, in a pensive mood, his eyes fixed on one object, at times looking slowly round him, as if to implore compassion. Garrick was often present at this scene of misery, and was ever after used to say, that it gave him the first idea of King Lear's madness.

This writer has often seen him rise in company to give a representation of this unfortunate father. He leaned on the back of a chair, seeming with parental fondness to play with a child, and, after expressing the most heart-felt delight, he suddenly dropped the infant, and instantly broke out in a most violent agony of grief, so tender, so affecting and pathetic, that every eye in company was moistened with a gush of tears. There it was, said Garrick, that I learned to imitate madness; I copied nature, and to that owed my success in *King Lear*.

So much for one aspect of what we may fairly assume to have been the greatest performance of Garrick's career. Other commentators have left their impressions on record, from which it is clear that the unhappy madman cannot have been Garrick's only model for this part. Here, for example, is Macklin's account:

The curse exceeded all imagination, and had such an effect that it seemed to electrify the audience with horror . . . whilst he exhibited such a sense of the pathetic on discovering Cordelia as drew tears of commiseration from the whole house.

John O'Keefe, on the other hand, was especially struck by Garrick's rendering of the old king's sudden recollection of his own want of power at the passage: 'I will do such things—what they are yet I know not; but they shall be the terror of the earth' —another stroke of pathos which can hardly have derived from Leman Street, since the words are spoken while Lear is still in possession of his five wits.

The fact that these three commentators should single out three quite different passages for praise is one more tribute to that quality in Garrick which most astonished his contemporaries—his many-sidedness. Whether he was the greatest actor that ever appeared on our stage must always be a matter of opinion, but there can hardly be a doubt that he was the most variously gifted. Goldsmith's 'epitaph', from which two or three lines have already been quoted, brings this out, and is worth printing at some length here as an estimate of character which has been generally held to be fair, though it touches Garrick's virtues rather more lightly than his faults:

> Here lies David Garrick. Describe me, who can,
> An abridgement of all that was pleasant in man.
> As an actor, confessed without rival to shine;
> As a wit, if not first, in the very first line:
> Yet, with talents like these and an excellent heart
> The man had his failings, a dupe to his art.
> Like an ill-judging beauty his colours he spread
> And beplastered with rouge his own natural red:
> On the stage he was natural, simple, affecting:
> 'Twas only that when he was off he was acting.
> With no reason on earth to go out of his way

He turned and he varied full ten times a day
Though secure of our hearts, yet confoundedly sick
If they were not his own by finessing and trick.
He cast off his friends as a huntsman his pack
For he knew, when he pleased, he could whistle them back.
Of praise a mere glutton, he swallowed what came,
And the puff of a dunce, he mistook it for fame;
Till his relish grown callous almost to disease
Who peppered the highest was surest to please.

Yet even more striking than his many-sidedness as a man was his versatility as an actor. Side by side with the power which made Fielding say, 'I regard [Garrick] in tragedy to be the greatest genius the world has ever produced', he had comic gifts of the highest order. He was also a notable mimic, and as Bayes in Buckingham's *The Rehearsal* was accustomed to point his contempt for old-school acting with a remarkably close burlesque of some of its practitioners. Most surprising of all, perhaps, in a player of strong individuality, he was an impersonator. Many great players —perhaps most great players—are so strongly themselves that they interpret each new part that they play in terms of their own personalities, leaving the arts of disguise to those who are to-day called, in a clumsy and misleading phrase, 'character actors', (clumsy because all good actors are character actors). Garrick loved disguise, and made it one of the chief weapons in his armoury. It was his delight, after having been sublimely unrecognizable as Lear one night, to be ridiculously unrecognizable as Abel Drugger the next. 'He represented the tobacco-boy', says Murphy, 'in the truest comic style: no grimace, no starting, no wild gesticulation. He seemed to be a new man.'

Versatility is a dangerous gift, for it not uncommonly leads its possessor to dissipate his powers instead of concentrating them on the highest aim within his range. Fielding, in the passage quoted above, seems to deplore that his friend Garrick 'sometimes condescends to play the fool', but is in no fear that his greatness in tragedy will suffer thereby. In this matter, as in others, Garrick made his own rules. And though it is now 170 years since he died, nothing has yet happened to invalidate the prophecy made by Alexander Pope when, as a very old man, he was taken to see one of Garrick's early performances and said that he was afraid the young man might be spoiled, for he would never have a competitor.

Chapter 6

'A WOMAN SIDDONS'

SOMETIME IN THE SUMMER OF 1775, MOODY, THE STOUT-hearted actor who had so delighted Garrick by his behaviour during the Fitzpatrick riots, happened to be playing in Liverpool, and Garrick wrote to ask him: 'Have you ever heard of a woman Siddons, who is strolling about somewhere near you?'

What Moody replied is not in evidence, and indeed it is likely that Garrick's information as to the woman Siddons's whereabouts was even vaguer than he made it seem, for early in August he had located her at Cheltenham and had asked another of his friends to report on her on his way to the races at Worcester. This friend was the Reverend Harry Bate, a sporting parson of the eighteenth-century pattern, who did not allow clerical duties to interfere unduly with worldly pursuits, and was editor of the *Morning Post* and knew his theatre well.

On 12 August Bate wrote to Garrick from the Hop Pole at Worcester:

MY DEAR FRIEND

After combatting the various difficulties of one of the cussedest cross-roads in this kingdom, we arrived safe at Cheltenham on Thursday last, and saw the theatrical heroine of that place in the character of Rosalind. Though I beheld her from the side wing of the stage (a barn about three yards over), and consequently under almost every disadvantage, I own she made so strong an impression upon me, that I think she cannot fail to be a valuable acquisition to Drury Lane. Her figure must be remarkably fine, although marred for the present.[1]

Her face (if I could judge from where I saw it) is one of the most strikingly beautiful for stage effect that I ever beheld, but I shall surprise you more when I assure you that these are nothing to her action and general stage deportment, which are remarkably pleasing and characteristic; in short, I know no woman who marks the different passages and transitions with so much variety, and at the same time propriety of expression. In the latter humbug scene with Orlando previous to her revealing herself, she did more with it than anyone I ever saw, not even your divine Mrs Barry excepted.

It is necessary after this panegyric, however, to inform you that her voice

[1] Her second child, Maria Sarah, was born on 5 November.

struck me at first as rather dissonant, and I fancy, from the private conversation I had with her, that in impassioned scenes it must be somewhat grating;
however, as I found it wear away as the business became more interesting, I am
inclined to think it only an error of affectation, which may be corrected, if not
totally removed.

She informed me she has been upon the stage from her cradle. This, though
it surprised me, gave me the highest opinion of her judgement, to find she had
contracted no strolling habits, which have so often been the bane of many a
theatrical genius. She will most certainly be of great use to you, at all events,
on account of the great number of characters she plays, all of which, I venture
to assert, she fills with propriety, though I have yet seen her in but one . . . I
should not wonder, from her ease, figure, and manner, if she made the proudest
she of either house tremble in genteel comedy—nay, beware yourself, Great
Little Man, for she plays Hamlet to the satisfaction of the Worcestershire critics.

The moment the play was over I wrote a note to her husband (who is a
damned rascally player, though seemingly a very civil fellow), requesting an
interview with him and his wife, intimating at the same time the nature of my
business. You will not blame me for making this forced march in your favour,
as I learnt that some of the Covent Garden Mohawks were intrenched near the
place and intended carrying her by surprise. At the conclusion of the farce they
waited upon me, and, after I had opened my commission, she expressed herself
happy at the opportunity of being brought out under your eyes, but declined
proposing any terms, leaving it entirely with you to reward her as you thought
proper.

You will perceive that at present she has all that diffidence usually the first
attendant on merit; how soon the force of Drury Lane examples, added to the
rising vanity of a stage heroine, may transform her, I cannot say. It happens
very luckily that the company comes to Worcester for the race week, when I
shall take every opportunity of seeing her, and if I find the least reason to alter
my opinion (perhaps too hastily formed), you shall immediately have my recantation. My wife, whose judgement in theatrical matters I have a high opinion
of, joins with me in these sentiments respecting her merit.

A week later, after hearing from Garrick, Bate followed this up,
not with a recantation but a confirmation; and in the meantime
he had to some extent revised his original downright rejection of
William Siddons's acting:

He requires only to be employed in any manner you shall think proper; and
as he is much more tolerable than I thought him at first, it may be no very
difficult matter to station him so as to satisfy the man, without burdening the
property. I saw him the other evening in *Young Marlow*, and then he was far
from despicable. . . . A jealousy prevailing through the theatre, upon a suspicion of their leaving them, the acting manager seems determined that I
shall not see her again in any character wherein she might give me a second
display of her theatrical powers.

She gave him something else, however—a list of the characters
she could play, with her favourite parts underlined. These parts

were Alicia in Rowe's *Jane Shore*, the Grecian Daughter in Murphy's tragedy of that name, Belvidera in *Venice Preserved*, Lady Townley in Vanbrugh's *Provoked Husband*, Portia, Rosalind, and the Widow Brady. And at the end of his letter Bate adds:

I forgot to tell you that Mrs Siddons is about twenty years of age. It would be unjust not to remark one circumstance in favour of them both; I mean the universal good character they have preserved here for many years, on account of their public as well as private conduct in life.

Garrick was fortunate in his talent-scout, who very clearly knew a good actress when he saw her; and he had a second opinion from his colleague and manager King, who went down to Cheltenham and saw Mrs Siddons in *The Fair Penitent*. He agreed that the Siddonses should join the Drury Lane Company as soon as possible after Sarah's child should be born. He arranged for an advance of cash to tide her over the confinement, and he offered her five pounds a week as salary—a handsome sum for an unknown country actress, considering that Mrs Abington and Mrs Yates were being paid no more than ten. When she joined the company he paid her so much attention that the older actresses were jealous. He evidently thought that he had made a great discovery, and that his new actress had only to appear to be acclaimed.

And then, she failed, disappointing both Garrick's high hopes and her own deeply felt, though carefully hidden, confidence that she had only to be given a chance in order to step, as Garrick himself had done nearly thirty-five years before, to the head of her profession.

Out of the list of favourite parts that she had given to Bate, Garrick had chosen Portia for her début, King playing Shylock. It was a good and tactful choice, for it gave her a clear chance to show her talent without embroiling her with any of her resentful rivals. *The Merchant of Venice* had not been acted in London for two years, and so the part of Portia was not the prescriptive property of any other actress. Somehow she let the chance slip, and made almost no impression at all. From the newspaper accounts next morning we get an impression of an appalling attack of stage-fright, brought on by physical weakness and a sense of inadequacy to the occasion. The notices are not unkind; they are something much worse—detached and dismissive. She was very pretty, her features were expressive, she had a fine stage figure and was uncommonly graceful, her words were delivered with good sense; but she tottered rather than walked, was unbecomingly dressed, could not be clearly heard, and had no fire or spirit. To sum up, a fragile, appealing young creature, but an awkward and provincial actress. *The Morning Post*, which had something of a vested interest in her through Bate, served her better than this, and there was an admission that the Trial Scene had not gone for nothing. Nowhere, however, is there a sign that the newcomer had fired the imagination even of a few discerning members of her first audience. Nor did she do much better when the play was repeated, a few nights later. Indeed, the whole season was a series of mortifications. Bate had reported that she had a 'very good breeches figure', and she was tried in the name-part of Jonson's *Epicœne*; but the critics found it tiresome that the Silent Woman who in the play turns out to be a boy should in fact be a woman. She then appeared in a play by Bate himself, but there was a riot and the piece was withdrawn. Finally, Garrick, now acting a round of farewell performances, gave her two chances, as Mrs Strickland to his Ranger in *The Suspicious Husband* and as Lady Anne to his Richard III. There is evidence that she did reasonably well in the former part, but in the latter she was thrown off her balance by the force with which Garrick played Richard, made mistakes which any novice could have avoided, and ended her season disastrously.

Still Garrick stood by her, and told her to go off to her summer engagement at Birmingham with the assurance that he would see to it that the new managers—Sheridan, Linley, and Ford—would re-engage her for the coming London season. He failed to do so, and during her engagement at Birmingham she received an official letter from Drury Lane telling her that her services were no longer required. This was worse than a wound to her vanity; it was a damaging blow to her self-confidence. Not yet mature enough to admit to herself that she had deserved nothing better, she blamed Garrick as a false friend (even accusing him of making her appear as Portia, 'a character in which it was not likely that I should excite any great sensation', with a convenient forgetfulness that the part had been underlined as one of her favourites on her own list), and continued to feel bitter against him for the rest of her life. 'He let me down,' she wrote long after, 'after all these protestations, in the most humiliating manner.'

It seems unlikely in the last degree that Garrick did anything of the kind. He had showed that, in spite of her failure to impress the town, he still believed in Sarah Siddons, and there is no real evidence that anybody else at Drury Lane shared his feeling. On the other hand, there is very good presumptive evidence that Sheridan did not share it, for it was not until six years later, in the face of her growing fame and in spite of a good deal of pressure, that he would consent to give her a second chance in London. Once she had become his leading lady, it was necessary for him to explain away his neglect or prejudice, which he did by blaming Garrick, who was now dead. Mrs Siddons, very ready to accept any explanation which exonerated her youthful self, believed this story, but we need not. Nobody ever knew better than Sheridan how to manage an actress, or was more calmly ready to flatter an offended tragedy queen into friendliness by telling her anything he thought she would like to hear. He told Mrs Siddons that Garrick had spoken disparagingly of her, and must have been jealous; and as she never at any time had the least spark of humour about herself, she found the explanation entirely satisfactory. On the face of things, a much more likely explanation is that Garrick kept his promise to suggest her re-engagement, but found himself unable to press the point when he realized that Sheridan thought nothing of her.

The real truth of the matter was that Garrick made his discovery too early. The 'woman Siddons' was no mere promising recruit, but a transcendent genius in the making, with all the uncompromising qualities which that term entails. For all her wide range of parts and her triumphant successes before country audiences she was, at twenty, quite undeveloped. Conscious of the power within her, she did not realize how entirely lacking she was in resource and control, without which she was apt to stultify herself by the very depth of her emotions. A genius has further to go than other artists, often along a harder road. It may be fairly claimed on her behalf that she was unlucky in the timing of her first big chance, so soon after the birth of her child, so little before Garrick's withdrawal from management; but it may also be seriously suggested that it was better for her in the end that success in London did not come too soon.

She went back to the life of a provincial strolling or 'stock' actress, which, with one or two short intermissions, was the only life she had ever known. It was neither a sordid nor a degrading life as she knew it, for her father, Roger Kemble, and Sarah Ward, his formidable wife, were self-respecting and respectable people. Snubs and slights had to be faced, of course, for prejudice against the theatre ran high in some of the country towns and a player was of less social consequence than a footman. But the Kembles, or at any rate the parents and their elder children, bore themselves like people sure of their own claim to good treatment, and generally got it.

That Sarah Siddons herself had something in her bearing that singled her out even in her youth, there is ample proof. The headmistress of a school for young ladies at Worcester accepted her as a pupil for a time, refusing any payment; and though the other girls began by cold-shouldering the player's daughter they came round in the end in admiration of her taste and skill when a school play was produced. Later on, when she and William Siddons first announced that they were in love with one another, her mother sent her to Mrs Greatheed, of Guy's Cliff in Warwickshire, to act as lady's maid to Lady Mary Bertie, a daughter-in-law of the house. Sarah was barely seventeen at the time, but already carried herself like a queen. Lady Mary used to say in after years that whenever her maid had come to attend her she had felt an almost irresistible inclination to stand up. During the short time Sarah was in this house she made for herself a curious betwixt-and-between position, sometimes reciting bits of plays for the entertainment of the servants' hall, sometimes reading to the family. (It is pleasant to notice that she remained on terms of friendship with the Greatheeds all her life, and a note in the diary of a guest at Guy's Cliff nearly half a century later records that Mrs Siddons and her daughter were staying in the house, and that Mrs Siddons gave a wonderful reading from *Othello*.)

Back in the provinces, then, and on familiar ground, she very quickly regained her self-confidence. In her Birmingham engagement, which lasted through the summer of 1776, she had the advantage of playing opposite that very competent actor John Henderson, who was so struck with her quality that he wrote to Palmer of Bath suggesting that he should engage her. Palmer was impressed, but had no vacancy to offer, and she acted that winter in Liverpool and Manchester, and then went on to York and played a season under Tate Wilkinson's management.

Wilkinson was now a much more respectable citizen than the irresponsible youth whose talent for mimicry had got him so disliked in London, but he still felt spiteful about Garrick, as his memoirs show, and would certainly not be the man to minimize Mrs Siddons's sense of grievance against Drury Lane or its managers. Indeed, it is pretty certain that he did precisely the opposite, for he tells with unction of the surprise that was felt in York that 'such a voice, such a judgement and such acting should have been neglected by a London audience, and by the first actor in the world'.

He tried to tempt his new leading lady to join his permanent company, but an offer from Palmer of Bath, which she now received, was obviously much more advantageous.

Bath was then, theatrically speaking, the second city of England. Still the favourite health resort of rank and fashion, it had an audience as sophisticated as that of Drury Lane. Nothing that happened in Bath was unknown or unremarked in London. What was more, Sheridan and his father-in-law, Linley, both active in the management of Drury Lane, had been Bath residents and were still in constant touch with the town. There could be no better base from which a determined, solemn young woman with a rankling grievance and a steadily increasing sense of power could conduct a campaign against London.

It took her four years, for first she had to conquer Bath. Here is her account of the process:

> I now made an engagement at Bath. Here my talents and industry were encouraged by the greatest indulgence, and, I may say, with some admiration. Tragedies which had been almost banished, again resumed their proper interest; but I had the mortification of being obliged to personate many subordinate characters in comedy, the first being in the possession of another lady. This I was obliged to submit to, or to forfeit part of my week's salary, which was only three pounds a week. Tragedies were now becoming more fashionable. While I laboured hard, I however earned a reputation.[1]

At last that reputation grew to a point at which an invitation to London was inevitable. It came in the summer of 1782, and it seems that Henderson, who had been the means of her arrival at Bath, was the immediate cause of her departure from it; for it was his report, after playing Benedick to her Beatrice, that finally decided Sheridan and Linley that her claim to real eminence was now good.

We need feel no surprise that her first reaction to the invitation, now that it had come, was a reluctance to accept. In Bath she had an assured position, a faithful public, and many good friends. To go to London was to risk that position, for another failure at Drury Lane would brand her for ever as second-rate. In this un-

[1] From *The Reminiscences of Sarah Kemble Siddons 1773-1785*, ed. by Wm. Van Lennep, 1942, taken from a long-lost, recently discovered manuscript now in the Harvard Library.

certainty of mind she may have suggested some compromise which would not entail a complete severance with Bath, for in a letter to a friend she says: 'I have the pleasure to inform you that I shall not go to London this winter. Mr Linley thinks my making a partial appearance will neither benefit myself nor the proprietors.'

However, go she did in the end; and on 10 November 1782, she appeared as Isabella in Southerne's *The Fatal Marriage*, and had one of the greatest triumphs in the history of the London stage. Her own spontaneous, excited account, written to her friend Dr Whalley, a wealthy clergyman who preferred writing bad poetry at Bath to looking after a parish, shows what it meant to her:

My Dear, Dear, Friend,

The trying moment is passed, and I am crowned with a success which far exceeds even my hopes. God be praised! . . . As I know it will give you pleasure, I venture to assure you I never in my life heard such peals of applause. I thought they would not have suffered Mr Packer to end the play. Oh! how I wished for you last night, to share a joy which was too much for me alone! My poor husband was so agitated that he durst not venture near the house . . . I have suffered tortures for [*sic*] the unblest these three days and nights past, and believe I am not in perfect possession of myself at present; therefore excuse, my dear Mr Whalley, the incorrectness of this scrawl, and accept it as the first tribute of love (after the first decisive moment) from your ever grateful and truly affectionate,

S. SIDDONS.

The play was repeated for eight nights, and the excitement grew night by night. Footmen sent out to buy tickets for their mistresses took up their positions at dawn and lay sleeping outside the theatre. Playgoers who did their own waiting for places had breakfast near the theatre and cheerfully spent the day in the crush. Night after night the actress played to audiences of tired people who shed their weariness the instant she appeared. The management did her every honour in its power, moving her at once, she says, 'from my very indifferent and inconvenient dressing-room to one on the stage-floor, instead of climbing a long staircase; and this room (oh, unexpected happiness!) had been Garrick's dressing-room'. Her original salary of five pounds a week was raised during the season to twenty, and her first benefit brought her in eight hundred pounds. From that time onwards she was the acknowledged queen of the English stage, where in tragedy she has never had a rival.

She took success well, for she was a genuine artist and a woman of character. She accepted the public adulation for what it was

worth, and did not allow it to turn her head or to affect the quality
of her work. She put on no airs except those which were natural
to her. But she was not much liked, for she had no humour and
little tact. Theatrical Bohemia could not feel about her, as it had
about Garrick, that she was not of the blood, but it could and did
bring the same charges against her as Garrick had had to face, that
she was mean and a snob. The second charge can be dismissed; she
found her friends in every class, and was faithful to them. The
imputation of stinginess, however, had something in it. She was
much fonder of money than Garrick had ever been, though she
had an excuse which Garrick could not have put forward, that it
was for her children that she was putting by.

She took motherhood as solemnly as she took her art. Indeed,
seeing what intense sincerity she brought to her work, it is fair
to say that the Mother was the best part she played, for she undoubtedly dramatized herself in relation to her children. It was
for her children, she told the playgoers of Bath, that she accepted
the Drury Lane invitation. She told them this at her farewell Bath
performance, in a correct but pedestrian epilogue of her own composition; and for good measure she had her three children on the
stage, addressed them rhetorically as 'Ye elves', and bade them
plead their mother's cause. An embarrassing scene, to the modern
mind, but perhaps it did not seem so to the Age of Sensibility; at
any rate, Bath had no ironical comment to offer.

It was for her children's security, not her own aggrandizement,
that she set herself a target of money to be saved, and if she
grudged spending money which might have brought that target
nearer it would be entirely in character. Her biographers have
made some attempt to make William Siddons her scapegoat here.
Since he was not a good enough actor to appear in her London
company, he had constituted himself a power behind her throne,
performing some of the duties which to-day would be shared by a
producer and a business manager. It is quite true that Siddons
often drove a hard bargain, but it is not really open to doubt that
his wife was as interested in the result as he was himself. It took
her only four years to reach her target, and she wrote at once to
the Whalleys to let them know:

I have at last, my friend, attained the ten thousand pounds which I set my heart
upon, and am now perfectly at ease with respect to fortune. I thank God who
has enabled me to procure myself so comfortable an income. I am sure my dear
Mrs Whalley and you will be pleased to hear this from myself.

Partly owing to this cause, and partly because she was thought to be too proud, she made herself deeply unpopular with the theatrical profession in the first years of her success. In Ireland especially she had to face popular disapproval. The Irish playgoers did not take to her fierce transports of passion, which had so little in common with Celtic melancholy, and she certainly did not take to Irish audiences; nor did it count in her favour that the Dublin Castle set took her up. She was admired but not liked, and finally made a false step which turned dislike into execration. She was invited to give a benefit performance for Digges, an old actor who had had a stroke and was in very low water, and she refused. Later, when she found that her refusal had caused widespread indignation, she changed her mind, got together a scratch company—the regular Dublin company were by now fulfilling an engagement at Limerick—and so saved her face. She never really lived this episode down, however, and in the end she probably paid more dearly than she deserved; but there is no doubt that her original impulse was an ungenerous one, particularly as stage people have an unwritten law that no help must be refused in such cases. Also, her own account of her conduct, written long after, is so patently disingenuous that it cannot be accepted.

In so short an account as this of Mrs Siddons's character it would be wrong to dwell too much on her less amiable qualities. She had the simple concentration of purpose which belongs to genius; in an inelastic nature, this is bound to cause offence, and in an actress the offence is bound to be exaggerated. According to her daughter Cecilia's account, the hard and calculating Mrs Siddons of the public imagination never existed. The real Sarah Siddons was, outside her work, a simple soul, credulous to a degree, never ready to suspect anybody, always trusting to appearances, and therefore apt to be influenced by people inferior to herself. It is a matter of common experience that people of this type, when they do find themselves deceived or let down, are out of all reason hard and unforgiving, so Cecilia's picture of her mother is probably true.

Chapter 7

TRAGEDY QUEEN

IT SEEMS PATENTLY ABSURD TO SAY THAT MRS SIDDONS, JOSHUA Reynolds's Tragic Muse, who with her brother, John Philip Kemble, restored declamation to the place in our theatre from which Garrick had deposed it, was a spontaneous and natural actress. Yet it was true. In her earliest days when her reputation was still in the making she was at the mercy of her temperament and could only do herself justice when she was in the mood. We have it from her own pen, early in her correspondence with the Whalleys:

I hope, with a fervency unusual upon such occasions, that you will not be disappointed in your expectations of me to-night; but sorry am I to say that I have often observed that I have performed worst when I most ardently wished to do better than ever. Strange perverseness! And this leads me to observe—as I believe I may have done before—that those who act mechanically are sure to be in some sort right; while we who trust to nature—if we do not happen to be in the humour (which, however, heaven be praised! seldom happens)—are dull as anything can be imagined, because we cannot feign.

This may be taken in conjunction with another passage in which she describes her own method of working herself into the skin of Constance in *King John*:

I never, from the beginning of the play to the end of my part of it, once suffered my dressing-room door to be closed, in order that my attention might be constantly fixed on those distressing events which, by this means, I could plainly hear going on upon the stage, the terrible effects of which progress were to be represented by me. Moreover, I never omitted to place myself, with Arthur in my hand, to hear the march, when, upon the reconciliation of England and France, they enter the gates of Angiers to ratify the contract of marriage between the Dauphin and the Lady Blanche, because the sickening sounds of that march would usually cause the bitter tears of rage, disappointment, betrayed confidence, baffled ambition, and, above all, the agonizing feelings of maternal affection to gush into my eyes.

This is not the place for a re-opening of the age-long discussion as to how much the player on the stage should feel of the emotion which he is acting. Probably the ideal solution is that he should feel the emotion at rehearsal and reproduce it in performance; but in practice it is probable that every player varies from one night to the next. There is a store of Garrick anecdotes, all purporting to show that for him, at any rate, feeling or the lack of it had no effect on performance, and Cumberland has one to the same effect about Mrs Siddons herself. No doubt experience and control have much to do with it—the old hand can produce by imitation an effect that the young one can only equal by a worked-up emotion. Also it is possible that in the specific case of Constance an actress is well advised to follow Mrs Siddons's example and work herself up, for the part is a very short one, and in the big scene it starts off at a high emotional pitch. Perhaps the modern Constances, who almost always fail to carry off that scene, would do well to copy Mrs Siddons's thorough methods. The point is interesting, but can only be discussed with real profit by actors. Here it is used only to show with what vehemence and sincerity Mrs Siddons went about her work.

In respect of her greatest part, Lady Macbeth, she has left us a very revealing document—the account of her feelings when, as a young actress, she first read the play.

It was my custom to study my characters at night, when all the domestic care and business were over. On the night preceding that in which I was to appear in this part for the first time, I shut myself up as usual, when all the family were retired, and commenced my study of Lady Macbeth. As the character is very short, I thought I should soon accomplish it. Being then only twenty years of age, I believed, as many others do believe, that little more was necessary than to get the words into my head; for the necessity of discrimination, and the development of character, at that time of my life, had hardly entered into my imagination.

This, by the way, is a naïve confession. It was at the age of twenty that she had her first chance at Drury Lane, and here she gives the best of all reasons why she failed to take that chance. But (as she says) to proceed:

But to proceed. I went on with tolerable composure, in the silence of the night (a night I never can forget), till I came to the assassination scene, when the horrors of the scene rose to a degree that made it impossible for me to get further. I snatched up my candle, and hurried out of the room in a paroxysm of terror. My dress was of silk, and the rustling of it, as I ascended the stairs to go to bed, seemed to my panic-stricken fancy like the movement of a spectre pursuing me. At last I reached my chamber, where I found my husband fast asleep. I clapped my candlestick down upon the table, without the power of putting the candle out, and I threw myself on my bed without daring to stay even to take off my clothes.

Here, surely, is the birth-pang of the tremendous performance she was to give ten years later. The girl of twenty could not have come near that performance, but it was what she had felt on that night she could never forget that the woman of thirty reproduced at Drury Lane.

An incident of the *Macbeth* first night—the date was 2 February 1785—shows how fresh was the mind which she brought to new parts at that time. Just as she was dressed, Sheridan came knocking at her door, and refused to listen to her plea to be left alone at this stressful moment. Reluctantly, she let him in:

What was my distress and astonishment when I found that he wanted me, even at this moment of anxiety and terror, to adopt another mode of acting the sleeping scene! He told me that he had heard with the greatest surprise and concern that I meant to act it without holding the candle in my hand; and when I argued the impracticability of washing out that 'damned spot' that was certainly implied by both her own words and those of her gentlewoman, he insisted that if I did put the candle out of my hand it would be thought a presumptuous innovation, as Mrs Pritchard had always retained it in hers. My mind, however, was made up, and it was then too late to make me alter it, for I was too agitated to adopt another method.

My deference for Mr Sheridan's taste and judgement was, however, so great, that, had he proposed the alteration whilst it was possible for me to change my own plan, I should have yielded to his suggestion; though even then it would have been against my own opinion, and my observation of the accuracy with which somnambulists perform all the acts of waking persons.

The scene, of course, was acted as I had conceived it, and the innovation, as Mr Sheridan called it, was received with approbation. Mr Sheridan himself came to me after the play, and most ingenuously congratulated me on my obstinacy.

These glimpses of the actress in relation to her work are enough to show how little regard we need pay in this place to the stately Mrs Siddons of legend, the stagey old actress who spoke blank verse to servants ('You've brought me water, boy: I asked for beer'), and wrote a great deal of quasi-intellectual stuff about her ponderings over Lady Macbeth and her other parts. The Mrs Siddons with whom we are concerned was a simple young woman with average intelligence; she acted as she felt, and she felt deeply.

Her acting was, then, a direct assault on the emotions of her audience, and she was in consequence even more dependent than other great players on response from her audience. Betterton, as Cibber tells us, did not much care for applause. He knew that he had technical tricks at his disposal with which he could surprise an audience into applause at any moment, and in consequence the only sign of response that he valued was complete, still silence. Mrs Siddons, one concludes, had no tricks of the kind, and a silent audience disconcerted her because she was not used to it.

After her retirement—characteristically, she settled the date of this event long in advance; she would leave the stage as soon as she had enough money to be able to afford a carriage—she used to give readings, at first in public, later privately, to friends. Maria Edgeworth was present at one of these, and has left a description:

I heard Mrs Siddons read at her town house a portion of *Henry VIII*. I was more struck and delighted than I ever was with any reading in my life. This is feebly expressing what I felt. I felt that I had never before fully understood, or sufficiently admired, Shakespeare, or known the full powers of the human voice and the English language. Queen Katharine was a character peculiarly suited to her time of life and to reading. There was nothing that required gesture or vehemence incompatible with the sitting attitude. The composure and dignity, and the sort of suppressed feeling, and touches, not bursts, of tenderness, of matronly, not youthful, tenderness, were all favourable to the general effect. I quite forgot to applaud—I thought she was what she appeared. The illusion was perfect, till it was interrupted by a hint from her daughter or niece, I forget which, that Mrs Siddons would be encouraged by having some demonstration given of our feelings. I then expressed my admiration, but the charm was broken.

It is easy to understand Miss Edgeworth's irritation, but with a little more sympathetic understanding of the actress's temperament she might have been less acid. Those were days, however, in which literary ladies did not have very much to do with actresses, and were apt to be artless about them. Fanny Burney, for example, meeting Mrs Siddons about the time of her retirement, expresses a naïve disappointment that she is not in private life all that she appears on the stage:

I expected her to have been all that is interesting; the delicacy and sweetness with which she seizes every opportunity to strike and to captivate upon the stage had persuaded me that her mind was formed with that peculiar susceptibility which, in different modes, must give equal powers to attract and delight in common life. But I was very much mistaken. As a stranger I must have admired her noble appearance and beautiful countenance, and have regretted that nothing in her conversation kept pace with her promise.

The ordinary playgoing public, however, was not so exacting as Miss Burney or so undemonstrative as Miss Edgeworth. It simply demanded of its favourite actress that she should be an actress, and it responded to her, in England at any rate, in a manner and to a degree that seems barely credible even to us who have seen that altogether incredible spectacle, mass hysteria over film stars who in some cases have no emotional equipment whatever.

Sarah Siddons's emotional equipment was her first, as it was her greatest, acting asset. She had it even as the young girl who believed that little more was necessary than to get the words of her part into her head. An incident during the Cheltenham season of 1774, a year before Bate discovered her, makes this clear. Cheltenham was then a very small town, but it was beginning to have some fame as a spa. One day the box-office keeper told Mrs Siddons that Lord Aylesbury had taken a box and was bringing some friends, adding that he had overheard enough to know that they were coming in hopes of getting a good laugh at the expense of a company of barn-stormers. That night the actress played her part—Belvidera in *Venice Preserved*—with all the power of which she was capable, and perhaps all the more strongly because of the atmosphere of antagonism which she felt, and the suppressed laughter which she thought she heard, from the Aylesbury box; for she never could bear to be made ridiculous. But next morning Lord Aylesbury met William Siddons in the street, congratulated him on his wife's acting, and told him that the ladies of his party had cried so hard that they were now all laid up with headaches. Later in the day his lordship's step-daughter recovered enough to be able to call on the actress; and according to Mrs Siddons's account it was Aylesbury who passed the word to Garrick that the young woman was something out of the common.

It was no doubt her special dependence on a responsive audience that caused her dislike for country engagements once she had become the rage in London. At Drury Lane she knew her public and could depend on it, but in the provinces she did not always get the quick sympathy she expected, and she tended to regard such engagements as little more than necessary, because lucrative, inflictions. In Ireland, as we have seen, she was never happy, and never succeeded in getting on terms with her audiences. She mourned unto them, but they would not weep. As for Edinburgh, her first experience there must have been one of the most disconcerting of her life.

Scottish audiences a hundred and fifty years ago were what they are now—blankly unresponsive till they have made up their minds to like a performance or a player, generous when they have. To face them is an ordeal to which some performers can never get used, for they find the feeling of hammering against a locked door so depressing that the warmth and light when—or if—the door is at last thrown open is not compensation enough. Mrs Siddons's first bid for admittance, as Belvidera in 1784, was all the more unrewarding because it was confidently made. She raged, she stormed, and the door remained grimly locked, with no sign that anybody was at home. 'Stupid people, stupid people!' she said (under her breath, luckily) and went to her bed, miserable and defeated. Next night was a repetition of the first, till she could bear it no longer and paused at the end of an impassioned speech, determined to get a response of some kind. 'That's no' bad!' said a judicial voice, and then, at last, came applause on the scale to which she was accustomed. The door was open.

She became the rage in Edinburgh to an extent that must have been embarrassing. One of her biographers, Mrs Kennard, records several instances of this—for example, that she once acted the sleep-walking scene in *Macbeth* to such continuous applause that she had to go through it again. Mrs Kennard adds that the ladies of Edinburgh had 'a fashionable mania' for hysterics and fainting when Mrs Siddons acted:

A distinguished surgeon, familiarly called 'Sandy Wood', who, with his shrewd common sense, had a way of seeing through the follies of his fashionable patients, was called from his seat in the pit, where he was to be found every evening Mrs Siddons acted, to attend upon the hysterics of one of the excitable ladies who were tumbling around him. On his way through the crowd a friend said to him, alluding to Mrs Siddons: 'This is glorious acting, Sandy.' Looking round at the fainting and screaming ladies in the boxes, Wood answered: 'Yes, and a d——d deal o't, too.'

This raises the question, often asked, just how much of the effect that Mrs Siddons made upon her audiences was due to the special susceptibility of the playgoers of her period, and how much to her own power; and its corollary, how great would be her effect upon modern audiences if she were an actress of to-day. People who ask these questions generally do so in the belief, tacit or confessed, that Sarah Siddons owes a great part of her fame not to her gifts but to the lucky accident that she appeared on the stage just as the public taste happened to want what she happened to have; that she was in fact not so great an actress as her contemporaries thought.

The answer I must give to that is that if Sarah Siddons appeared to-day and were dismissed—as she certainly would be in some quarters—as a 'ham' actress, the failure would lie not with her but with the age that rejected her. Once again, the actor is put at a disadvantage in comparison with other artists because he is his own medium of expression. Many a painter, composer, or writer now universally accepted as great has failed to seem great to the people of his own time; an actor's greatness must be recognized by his contemporaries or it can never be recognized at all.

To admit that Sarah Siddons was fortunate in living when she did is not, then, to doubt or detract from her greatness. Nor must it be forgotten that if the audiences before which she acted were specially and even ridiculously susceptible to the vehement emotions of classical tragedy, it was she who had made them so. Tragedy was very little in favour when she first appeared in London. There had been no notable revival of *The Fatal Marriage* for twenty-seven years before the day when she electrified London with it, and even *Venice Preserved* had been on the shelf since 1770. Yet by the end of her first season it was almost true to say that nobody any longer went to the theatre to laugh.

Apart altogether from the foolish ladies shrieking and fainting in the boxes, we have to remember that the age was one which, so far from being ashamed to show its feelings, actually took credit to itself for doing so. In 1787, for example, Sheridan's great speech against Warren Hastings produced such an effect on the House of Commons that Pitt adjourned the session so that a division could be taken on the morrow in cooler blood; and later in the year Sheridan's speech in Westminster Hall at Hastings's trial caused his first wife (Elizabeth Linley) to write to Sheridan's sister: 'It is impossible, my dear woman, to convey to you the delight, the astonishment, the adoration, he has excited in the breasts of every class of people. Even party prejudice has been overcome by a display of genius, eloquence and goodness which nobody with anything like a heart about them could have listened to without being the wiser and the better for the rest of their lives.' It certainly excited strong emotions in the breast of his leading lady, for she fainted and was carried out; and as people were paying up to £50 for their seats, it seems unlikely that she was putting on an act like some of her own admirers in the boxes.

Yet even with an audience thus keyed to emotion, the effects Mrs Siddons got were astonishing—astonishing not merely for what she made the spectators feel, but for what she made them believe. Probably the most extraordinary feat in this way of which the stage has any record was hers in the last act of Rowe's *Tamer-lane*. Aspasia, the heroine of this piece, sees her lover strangled before her eyes and then falls dead herself. Mrs Siddons gave such an exhibition of agony and horror in this scene that when she fell the audience thought she was dead in very truth, called for the curtain to be lowered, and could hardly be persuaded by the management's assurances that the actress had only been acting. And in case anybody feels inclined to belittle this achievement by suggesting that the audience must have been a collection of simpletons, it should be added that in that audience were two experienced theatre men, Holman the actor and the elder Macready, and that Holman said: 'Macready, do I look as pale as you?' Even after the audience was reassured that the actress was alive it refused to listen to the rest of the play.

Sometimes she had the same effect on her fellow-actors as Garrick as Richard III had had on her, years before. Young, acting Beverley to her Mrs Beverley in *The Gamester* at Edinburgh, once dried up completely at the very climax of his death-scene, and could not speak in spite of several prompts till Mrs Siddons touched him on the shoulder and said softly: 'Mr Young, recollect yourself.' He afterwards explained that she had thrown such grief into the line which should have been his cue that his throat swelled and he had been physically unable to speak. If this could be her effect on an experienced leading man, it is easy to believe that when as Queen Katharine in *Henry VIII* she turned on a small-part actor with:

> If I know you well
> You were the duke's surveyor, and lost your office
> On the complaint o' the tenants: take good heed
> You charge not in your spleen a noble person
> And spoil your nobler soul. I say, take heed;
> Yes, heartily, beseech you. . . .

her look was so menacing that the youth came off sweating and shaking and vowing that not for anything would he meet her eyes again. Henderson, who was responsible more than any other one man for getting her back to London when her full powers had ripened, committed himself to the boldly sweeping statement that she had never had an equal and would never have a superior.

One of her biographers, James Boaden, has preserved for us a contemporary description of the actress's physical and mental equipment which goes as far as such a catalogue may to account for her outstanding quality:

There never, perhaps, was a better stage figure than that of Mrs Siddons. Her height is above the middle size, but not at all inclined to the *embonpoint*. There is, notwithstanding, nothing sharp or angular in the frame; there is sufficient muscle to bestow a roundness upon the limbs, and her attitudes are, therefore, distinguished equally by energy and grace. The symmetry of her person is exact and captivating.

Her face is peculiarly happy, the features being finely formed, though strong, and never for an instant seeming overcharged, like the Italian faces, nor coarse and unfeminine under whatever impulse. On the contrary it is so thoroughly harmonized when quiescent, and so expressive when impassioned, that most people think her more beautiful than she is. So great, too, is the flexibility of her countenance, that the rapid transitions of passion are given with a variety and effect that never tire upon the eye.

Her voice is naturally plaintive, and a tender melancholy in her level speaking denotes a being devoted to tragedy; yet this seemingly settled quality of voice becomes at will sonorous or piercing, overwhelms with rage, or in its wild shriek absolutely harrows up the soul. Her sorrow, too, is never childish, her lamentation has a dignity which belongs, I think, to no other woman; it claims your respect along with your tears. Her eye is brilliant and varying like the diamond; it is singularly well placed . . . and has every aid from brows flexible beyond all female parallel, contracting to disdain, or dilating with the emotions of sympathy, or pity, or anguish. Her memory is tenacious and exact—her articulation clear and exact—her pronunciation systematic and refined.

Nor has nature been partially bountiful—she has endowed her with quickness of conception, and a strength of understanding equal to the proper use of such extraordinary gifts. So entirely is she mistress of herself, so collected, and so determined in gesture, tone, and manner, that she seldom errs, like other actors, because she doubts her powers of comprehension. She studies her author attentively, conceives justly, and describes with a firm consciousness of propriety. She is sparing in her action, because English nature does not act much. . . . No studied trick or start can be predicted; no forced tremulation of the figure, where the vacancy of the eye declares the absence of passion, can be seen; no laborious strainings at false climax, in which the tired voice reiterates one high tone beyond which it cannot reach, is ever heard; no artificial heaving of the breasts, so disgusting when the affectation is perceptible; none of those arts by which the actress is seen, and not the character, can be found in Mrs. Siddons.

So natural are her gradations and transitions, so classical and correct her speech and deportment, and so intensely interesting her voice, form, and features, that there is no conveying an idea of the pleasure she communicates by words. She must be seen to be known. What is still more delightful, she is an original; she copies no one living or dead, but acts from nature and herself.

This is so able a piece of writing that one wishes that Boaden, instead of explaining complacently that he has touched up its composition here and there, had given us its author's name. It gives a more vivid picture of Sarah Siddons than Cibber has been able to give us of Betterton, or anybody, even Lichtenberg, of Garrick;

yet even so the author realizes that he has not succeeded in captur-
ing her essence. 'She must be seen to be known'—it is the same cry,
generation after generation.

Yet there is one impression of her, written not by a professional
author but by that same actor, Charles Mayne Young, whom she
had once bereft of words on the stage at Edinburgh, which seems
to me to convey more clearly what she was than any composed
and carefully thought out word picture could do. It is a description of her as Volumnia, when she played that part to the
Coriolanus of her brother, John Philip Kemble:

I remember her coming down the stage in the triumphal entry of her son
Coriolanus, when her dumb show drew plaudits that shook the building. She
came alone, marching and beating time to the music; rolling (if that be not too
strong a term to describe her motion) from side to side, swelling with the triumph
of her son. Such was the intoxication of joy which flashed from her eye, and lit
up her face, that the effect was irresistible. She seemed to me to reap all the
glory of that procession to herself. I could not take my eye from her. Coriolanus,
banner, and pageant, all went for nothing to me, after she had walked to her
place.

Chapter 8

KEAN, THE SPOILT CHILD

IT IS SAID THAT IN THE KEMBLE FAMILY JOHN PHILIP WAS considered a finer player than his sister, Sarah. To us, enjoying the double advantage of perspective and detachment, this idea seems manifestly ridiculous. We are in no doubt at all that Sarah Siddons had genius, whereas John Philip Kemble could rise no higher than talent, environment, industry, and a majestic solemnity could take him. Yet something may be said for the Kemble view. John Philip came slowly to his artistic maturity, and by the time his powers were at their best hers may have been slightly on the wane. It is clear from her own words, already quoted, that in her heyday she got her effects not by reproducing emotions felt during study and rehearsal, but by working up an actual emotion before she went on the stage and discharging it full at her audience. So long as the actor can control himself while doing it, this is probably the most moving kind of acting: but it is not a kind that can be maintained throughout a long career. Sooner or later, when the sheer strength and energy needed for such a performance begin to fail, the player must find a way of making his effect without spending himself to the utmost.

Sarah Siddons must have learnt this lesson somewhere in her thirties, and as she matured she grew stately and majestic, like her brother. More and more she came to act in the style which, natural to him, was artificial to her, till by the time of her early retirement she had become merely one of twin pillars which carried the main weight of that awful edifice, the Kemble Tradition. Her niece, Fanny Kemble, herself an actress of fame, wrote of her 'Aunt Siddons' many years later in a tone curiously compounded of respect, amusement, and pity. By the time Fanny knew her aunt, tremendousness had become so ingrained a habit with her that she carried it unconsciously into private life; and we have Fanny's word for the truth of that famous story of the shopman who, having sold the Tragic Muse some material, was struck dumb with terror by the tone in which she asked him: 'But will it wash?'

The actress whose displays of spontaneous emotion had electrified her own generation became in the end almost as artificial as Cibber and Quin; the public, unconsciously seeking relief from the strained nobility of the Kemble school, was ripe for the arrival of a new great natural actor. And on 26 January 1814, Edmund Kean came to the rescue of the London stage much as Garrick had, upwards of seventy years before.

Kean was in almost every way a complete contrast to the Kembles, not merely on the stage but behind the scenes as well. They were innately respectable in their private lives, he seemed fated to disrepute. They were accepted by high society almost as equals, he took a defiant pleasure in low company. Their reputations never had a stain, and when a pair of swindlers whom Mrs Siddons had unwisely befriended rewarded her with slander and attempted blackmail, they could find nobody to believe their story. Kean's reputation was such that when he involved himself in a foolish scandal with another man's wife, in circumstances far from honourable to the other man, he was made the victim of a public persecution as relentless and as cruel as if he had been convicted of breaking every commandment in the decalogue. Only two qualities had he in common with the Kembles—his aptitude for the stage and his fierce personal pride: and his pride took the form, not of a grown man's self-respect but of a spoilt child's demand for special indulgence.

Throughout this book, with an iteration that may well have become wearisome, I have insisted that the actor's values are the values of a child, and that as a child he must be regarded if he is to be understood. Some readers not closely acquainted with the fascinating, lunatic world of the theatre may have thought that this was just a fanciful literary way of putting things, not meant to be taken as literal in any great degree. In case that may be so, I must give an assurance here that in the case of Edmund Kean at any rate I am using no figure of speech. Only if Kean is judged by the nursery's standards can he be sympathetically judged, or even understood at all. Judged by adult methods of appraisal—that is to say, by results—he was a deplorable person who misused great gifts, so that they were an untimely loss to the world. That was the verdict of his day, and in point of historical fact it was not an unjust verdict; but neither was it a kind or comprehending one. A more sympathetic society would have known that Kean was not so much a hardened, irreclaimable offender as a naughty and badly brought up child of the type, which, having done something clever and failed to excite the attention it thinks due to it, goes on to do something outrageous and is punished; and then, smarting under a sense of injustice, sets out deliberately to be as naughty as possible, secretly wishing all the time to be good.

Edmund Kean was not fortunate in his first biographers, or perhaps it would be fairer to say that the biographers were not fortunate in their subject. Kean's origin was doubtful and his childhood sordid; and he was deeply ashamed of both facts and tried to conceal them later by any fantastic invention that came into his head—as that he had been educated at Eton and had been an officer in the army. Besides the tales which he invented himself, other more plausible legends of his escapades and misdemeanours were commonly repeated, and many of these were accepted and included in accounts of his life. Not till 1933, exactly one hundred years after the actor's death, did any scientific attempt at establishing the facts appear, when Harold Newcomb Hillebrand published in New York an admirable piece of scholarship which, however, makes rather depressing reading as it continually reveals how many of the accepted 'facts' concerning Kean are based on hearsay and conjecture. Five years later Giles Playfair published a less meticulous study, accepting without explanation several of the stories which he knew had been rejected by Hillebrand, but contributing to his subject a most valuable reassessment of the character of Kean's wife, hitherto accepted by all writers—Hillebrand included—at her own valuation as a noble woman deeply wronged. Playfair maintains that Mary Kean, merely by being the wrong woman for Edmund, failed him almost as badly as he failed her. It is a conjecture solidly based on such facts as are known, and I shall adopt it here.

In a short sketch of Kean's life, designed not to sort out fact from fiction but only to show what kind of man he was, there is no room for careful documentation. The account of his career which follows, up to the time of his arrival at Drury Lane, must be taken as an approximation to the truth rather than truth—what his biographers think may have happened, rather than what actually did. Even his parentage is not established for certain, though it is clear that his heredity was all against him. His reputed father, another Edmund Kean, drove himself out of his wits and into a suicide's grave by drink at the age of twenty-two. His mother, Ann Carey, granddaughter of Henry Carey who wrote 'Sally in Our Alley', was a dissolute young woman to whom the birth of a bastard child was just an annoying interlude. She never showed any interest in her child except when there seemed to be a chance to make money out of him, and he was brought up by a small-part actress at Drury Lane named Charlotte Tidswell, mistress of Edmund's uncle, Morris Kean, who had some skill and reputation as a mimic.

It is easy to see where in this dubious ancestry the boy got his desire to act, but less easy to account for his absolute determination to cut a great figure in the world, his morbid pride, his abnormal sensitiveness to insult, fancied or real. These were qualities personal to himself, and they, together with his inherited passion for brandy, decided his fate. Again and again, when ambition, determination, and hard work had won him a deserved reward, pride and over-sensitiveness impelled him to throw that reward away, and he tried to find solace for his disappointment in drink and debauchery. His vices were the vices of a man, but his behaviour was that of a child; and it was while he was still a child that he began throwing his chances away.

At the age of about eleven he was befriended by a benevolent lady, a Mrs Clarke, who took him into her house, gave him good clothes, sent him to school, and—perhaps most important of all to Edmund—showed off his precocious talents to her friends. One of these friends, who had brought his wife and small daughters up from the country on a visit to the house, showed surprise when he found that Edmund was to be included in a theatre party that was being arranged. Edmund instantly got up from the dining-table, left the house, and was not seen for seven days, when a local ostler found him lying insensible on a dung-hill near by. It turned out that he had walked to Portsmouth and tried to enlist in the Navy; and, that failing, had returned with the intention of staging a spectacular death as near the house of his protectress as possible. After this escapade, Mrs Clarke lost her interest in him, and he drifted back to the life of a theatre child in Drury Lane. If he had had enough humility to swallow the insult offered him by Mrs Clarke's friend, his whole career might well have been different. But humility and self-discipline were not in him. He wanted to be treated as a gentleman and a leading actor before he had established his claim to respect in either capacity; he knew that he was destined to be great, therefore everybody else must recognize it too. He must be treated as a person of consequence in private, and he must not be required to play subordinate parts in public.

Most unfortunately for anybody with such a temperament, he had a great success as an infant prodigy, even appearing before George III at Windsor and reciting to the Eton boys. He was a tumbler and acrobat also, and in his early years on the regular stage the managers who engaged him did so for his skill as Harlequin and were not much impressed by his ambition to be a tragedian. There was little that he could not do, and success came to him easily in those first years, for he was playing leading parts in Samuel Jerrold's theatre at Sheerness, still dressed as a boy, in 1804. His salary was no more than fifteen shillings a week and he earned it hard, but it was a living wage and he was still a success. There can have been little doubt in his mind then that greater stages would yield to him with equal ease.

This was a bad preparation for nine years of struggle and disillusionment, and in consequence those years bore hard on him. Engagements at the Theatre Royal, Belfast, in 1805 (when he attracted the passing attention of Mrs Siddons) and at the Haymarket in 1806 showed him that the great stages were not, after all, going to be his without a bitter struggle. He made no deep impression on his audiences in the small parts allotted to him, and his fellow-actors laughed at his insignificant size—his height was only five feet three—and his attempts to make himself noticeable. Resentfully he flung off to the small theatres again, and after various engagements in Kent, including one in his old position at Sheerness, he went to Gloucester at the beginning of 1808 to act on a circuit which included Stroud, Cheltenham, and a number of other neighbouring towns. Here he made perhaps the most disastrous mistake of his whole mismanaged life. He fell in love with, and married, Mary Chambers, a woman nine years older than himself and a very poor actress. To have married at all at his age and in his position would have been foolish; to marry this particular woman was, or rather turned out later to have been, sheer insanity.

Mary Chambers was not in any sense a bad woman, and in the narrow sense was a very good woman indeed, for her virtue was unspotted and her presentability complete. She had come from a respectable Irish home to be a governess in England; and how, with no real bent for the stage, she came to be a strolling player at the age of twenty-eight is something of an unsolved mystery.

MRS SARAH SIDDONS (1755–1831)
as Lady Macbeth, from the portrait by G. H. Harlowe

EDMUND KEAN (1787–1833)
as Sir Charles Overreach, from the painting by William Hook Morley

Her one professional asset was that she looked and spoke like a lady, and the unexpectedness of this in such surroundings gave her her first appeal for Kean. She on her side found him equally unexpected. His brilliant dark eyes, the fine though rather too elaborate manners which he could assume when he chose, his air of being somebody, marked him out at once. She made what seems like a dead set at him, flattering him with the open admiration which he had not enjoyed since his days as an infant prodigy. This gave him the self-confidence which as a rule he could find only in the tavern, and he talked freely to her of his hopes and ambitions; and soon she believed as completely as he did in his great destiny. We need not put Mary down as a conscious schemer. No doubt she was fascinated and thought herself in love with this wayward genius of nineteen, whom it was her mission to save from his worst self and support on his way to fame and riches. Underneath this, however, there must have been some calculation that in Edmund Kean she had her best, and probably at her age her last, chance of a marriage which might mean social advantage, just as on his side he must have reflected with satisfaction that here was a wife who would help him to his ambition to get himself accepted as a gentleman among gentlemen.

Almost from the first, the marriage began to fail. Edmund was what he was, and Mary lacked altogether the qualities that might have brought out the best in him. She had none of the gay gallantry of the good trouper, and though her belief in her husband's possibilities remained, it was soon overlaid with a resentful feeling that he was letting her down by throwing his talents away. She nagged, she complained, and she moaned, undermining his confidence and so sending him to the brandy bottle to restore his belief in himself. But though he was drinking heavily, she had to admit that he was working hard. He was determined to be a tragedian, and a great one, and to this end, in Mary's own words, 'he studied and slaved beyond any actor I ever knew'. He would take long solitary walks, thinking out the parts he would one day play in London; but meanwhile his difficulty was to be allowed to play them at all. Managers did not 'see' this shabby little man with the brilliant eyes in tragic parts. Tragedians were big, strong, handsome, and declamatory men, like John Philip Kemble. Even when Kean did play the parts, the country critics failed to be impressed. Playfair quotes a notice from *The Staffordshire Advertiser*, written about a year after the marriage, during a season at Lichfield:

D

Mr Kean, who has been figuring here as the principal tragic hero, is another example of the blundering folly of misplacing of which we see so many in the country theatres. Without energy, dignity or the advantages of a voice, he dragged through the heroic scenes with a dull monotony oppressive to himself and doubly so to the audience. He appears to understand his author, but the effects of a clear conception are totally lost in the natural defects of his voice and person. This performer's genius is nevertheless of an elevated cast—he is a good Harlequin!

That notice is well put, but it is the product of a closed mind. Obviously, to the writer, little men with brilliant eyes and no organ-boom in their voices were simply not acceptable as tragic heroes. On the other hand, if the 'dull monotony' of which Kean is accused was not prejudiced opinion but objective fact, there is the possibility that Kean, faced by an unresponsive audience which he despised, had no heart in his work.

Playfair quotes Macready in an attempt to prove that at this point in his career Kean was not a good actor:

A little mean-looking man in a shabby green satin dress (I remember him well) appeared as the hero, Alonzo the brave. It was so ridiculous that the only impression I carried away was that the hero and heroine were the worst in the piece. How little did I know, or could guess, that under the shabby green satin dress was hidden one of the most extraordinary theatrical geniuses that have ever illustrated the dramatic poetry of England.

'That impression', says Playfair, 'was not exaggerated or in-expert. Macready was the son of a provincial manager and had been brought up to know the stage. He was also a balanced and impartial critic.' Yes—but at the time when he saw this perform-ance he was not yet a balanced and impartial critic, but a school-boy; and even an intelligent schoolboy commonly judges not by what he sees but by what he has been told to look for. My own experience is that since I became a critic I have had to modify, or even reverse, nearly all my schoolboy judgements. And surely Mr Playfair, himself the son of an actor-manager of genius, must know that the offspring of a theatre-manager is more likely than other people to have preconceived notions of how acting should be done, and to dismiss with youthful scorn any performance that does not fit those notions. The possibility that young Macready on this occasion was dismissing Kean merely because he was not in the least like Kemble is too strong to be set aside.

This is not the place for a detailed account of Kean's wander-ings during the next four years, or of the gradual sapping of his belief in his high destiny. He continued to play to audiences which received his Hamlet with apathy and his Harlequin with vociferous delight. He continued to be high and mighty about the parts he played, till at last he lost an engagement in a characteristically foolish fashion. Some local bigwigs in Guernsey had asked for *The Royal Oak* to be performed, and Kean found himself cast against his inclination for Charles I. He went and got drunk, sent a message to say that King Charles had been beheaded on the way to the theatre, and followed this up by sitting in the auditorium and mocking at the manager, who was reading the part. The audience threw him out, and the manager fined him a fortnight's salary, which in the circumstances was magnanimous; but Kean, deeply insulted, threw up his position and his salary of two guineas a week.[1]

Now that he had a wife and family to support, such conduct was as monstrously silly as Mary thought it; and at last he admitted himself beaten. Only a few discriminating playgoers here and there had thought him fitted for tragedy—though on the whole the tone of his notices was improving—and already, in 1812, he had demeaned himself to ask humbly for a small-part engagement at Drury Lane, only to find his application ignored. There now seemed to be nothing for it but to leave Mary and the children in Exeter, to go up to London and see what his 'aunt', Charlotte Tidswell (who disliked Mary intensely), could do for him in London. She got him an engagement with Elliston, a leading actor in the Drury Lane company who was also a manager on his own account, and was about to reopen the Olympic Theatre in Wych Street in a few months' time. Kean rejoined his family, took a temporary engagement at Barnstaple to tide him over till Elliston was ready for him, and made up his mind to a future of dull safety, with his dream of greatness finally dissipated.

This is a literally true statement. The two great Patent Theatres of London, Drury Lane and Covent Garden, still enjoyed a monopoly of the right to present 'legitimate' drama in the London winter season, and when they closed in the summer the Haymarket took their place. At no other theatre could a player of Kean's type appear to much advantage; and in addition, by accepting an engagement at one of the minor theatres such as Kean had just arranged with

[1] This story is rejected by Hillebrand, and accepted without a qualm by Playfair. I print it here, not because I have any opinion as to its truth to fact, but because of its truth to character. Whether in this way or another, Kean did throw up his Guernsey engagement, and land his family penniless in Exeter.

Elliston, an actor automatically put himself out of the running for a place in the companies of any of the legitimate theatres, which blacklisted the minor theatres and recruited only from the country. It was about this time, while she was in Exeter, waiting for her husband's news that all his hopes of glory and hers of grandeur were at an end, that Mary Kean wrote a letter to her friend, Margaret Roberts, showing how utterly her faith in him had vanished:

My first step to misery was going on the stage. My character I preserved pure and unsullied. I then married my husband—possessed of every talent requisite for that profession, educated to give grace to that talent, and could he have endured patiently a little longer, fortune might have rewarded his very great abilities. To forget sorrow he first took to drinking. Every dissipation followed, of course. His nights were spent with a set of wretches—a disgrace to human nature. One step led to another, till inevitable ruin was the end.

The doleful past tense makes it clear that in her view nothing more was to be hoped from such a man. Yet within a month negotiations had begun which were to take him to Drury Lane, and within four he was London's idol and all England had heard of him as the great tragedian of his time.

How this came about so unexpectedly, and how near it came to falling through, makes a fascinating story in itself. Among the more discriminating playgoers who had seen Kean acting in the West Country, and had thought him not merely unusual but extraordinary, was a certain Dr Drury, late headmaster of Harrow. Drury found himself one day in company with Pascoe Grenfell, one of Samuel Whitbread's committee which was then running Drury Lane so ineptly that the great theatre, as everybody knew, was on the brink of ruin; and he talked glowingly of Kean's powers. Grenfell was impressed, and Drury wrote to Kean (whom he did not know personally) to tell him that there was a chance of a Drury Lane engagement for him. The news came at a singularly unhappy moment. The elder of the Kean children, Howard, a boy of four whom both his parents adored passionately, was very ill indeed, and money for doctors and treatment was desperately needed. Drury, wisely enough, had not encouraged extravagant hopes, and nothing more was heard from him; and at last Edmund, unable to bear the suspense and anxiety and feeling that if he delayed longer Elliston might withdraw his offer, wrote to Drury asking him to do anything he could to bring matters to a head. Drury got in touch with the Drury Lane authorities to such effect that he was able to write to Kean on 7 November 1813 a most encouraging letter, telling him that Drury Lane was seriously considering him.

This letter, delayed in the post, arrived on the 13th; but on the 11th, in his impatient despair, Kean had written to Elliston confirming his acceptance of the engagement at the Olympic (or Little Drury, as it was called). And on the 15th, acting at Dorchester to a miserably thin house, he noticed an attentive stranger in a box, who came round after the performance and introduced himself as Samuel Arnold, the Drury Lane manager. Arnold offered Kean an engagement, and confirmed the offer at breakfast next morning, the terms being eight pounds a week for the first year, nine pounds for the second, and ten pounds for the third. Kean, who had not slept all night for excitement, accepted at once. The fact that he was under contract to Elliston does not seem to have crossed his mind. If it did, he dismissed it with a spoilt child's assurance that nobody could be so unkind as to hold him to a promise. At all events, he said nothing to Arnold, and wrote off at once to Elliston, telling him what had happened, and added: 'It gives me unspeakable regret that the proposals did not reach me before I had commenced negotiations with you; but I hope, sir, you will take a high and liberal view of the question when I beg to decline the engagement for Little Drury. Another time I shall be happy to treat with you.' On 20 November, Arnold reported to the Drury Lane Committee that he had made a discovery in Kean, and that he had engaged him from the beginning of December 'on terms which he considered very advantageous to the theatre', and on the 21st Kean wrote a letter of excited gratitude to Dr Drury.

Then, when he was at the very peak of his hopes, everything began to go wrong. On the 22nd the child Howard died—unexpectedly, said his father in a second, short, grief-stricken letter to Drury—and was buried on the 24th. This kept Kean at Dorchester longer than he had intended, and by the time he reached London at the beginning of December he had had a letter from Elliston, written on 23 November, calling him 'a deserter' and warning him that the appeal to him to take a 'high and liberal view of the question' had failed. In spite of this he seems to have made up his mind that Elliston had no claim on him, for he reported quite happily at Drury Lane, was warmly welcomed by Arnold, and was paid his first week's salary. This enabled him to find himself some good rooms at 21 Cecil Street, where his wife joined him with their surviving son, Charles, a few days later. Then Elliston appealed to Drury Lane, and Kean found himself in real trouble.

A long, rambling account of the events which followed is contained in a letter sent by Kean to Dr Drury about the turn of the year. It is written with the purpose of showing his protector that he has been treated by Arnold and Elliston with monstrous cruelty and injustice, but its effect on one who reads it now, with knowledge of subsequent events, is quite different. It seems to me to show quite clearly that Arnold and Elliston must have put their heads together and decided to teach this spoiled child from the provinces a salutary lesson in behaviour. He had treated both of them with less than candour, and must be made to understand that honesty would have been a better policy. Arnold told him that while he was undoubtedly a member of Drury Lane, his engagement could not begin nor his salary be paid till he could show a written discharge from his obligation to Elliston; while Elliston was haughty on paper and elusive in person. When at last by frantic efforts Kean had secured an interview with both of them at the same time, Elliston talked Kean's head off and Arnold was heavily repressive. At last, when the punishment had continued for two weeks or more, Elliston (a known eccentric, who was probably enjoying the whole affair hugely by this time) suddenly relented for no reason that Kean could discern and promised to sign the necessary paper, on condition that Kean agreed to pay two guineas a week for an actor to take his place at the Olympic. Next day when the paper was to be signed, Elliston was elusive again and it took Kean five hours to run him to earth; after which Arnold, having kept him waiting for an hour in the passage outside his room, had him in and told him 'with the continued brow of severity' that he would have no claim on the treasury till the following week. The lesson was certainly a severe one, but it was not unmerited, for at the end of his self-exculpatory letter Kean asks Drury, in a tone of injury, whether it was reasonable to expect him to miss his chance of greatness merely because he had signed on with Elliston. The ordinarily honourable course of telling Arnold the exact position and getting him to arrange things with Elliston—who, as a Drury Lane member himself, would not have been likely to make difficulties—was at no time in Kean's mind.

On 28 December, Mary Kean, with her queer knack of always being at her most hopeless just before her fortunes were about to improve, wrote to her sister in Ireland:

Sad and melancholy ever is my theme to be at this happy season. While thousands are revelling in luxury I with many other forlorn ones shed the tears of misery—no hope now—no, no resource—cold, cold in the earth is that jewel that was my only consolation. . . . Though I know not where I shall be, or where we go, answer this as soon as possible, as I may get it, or it will be sent where I am. Little John [Charles Kean's other name] is not well. He too is a beautiful boy but should I lose him—I wish I knew in what manner to earn my bread or how I could get support. I have no one to apply to, for none will hear me. Oh that heaven would please to hear me and lay me by my boy—with my little John.

The day after this was written, Kean was called on to learn the last of his lesson. An actor from Ireland named Huddart was given a trial as Shylock, the very part in which it had been agreed that Kean's own Drury Lane début was to be made.

If Huddart had made a success, it is possible that Kean might have had to submit to still more discipline. But Huddart failed completely, and the Committee were reminded sharply that they did most desperately need a new actor, and that Arnold still thought Kean their best chance. The Drury Lane company learned that the 'little man in the capes', at whose insignificant figure and tragic eyes they had been laughing for the past three weeks, was to make *his* appearance as Shylock; and on 26 January 1814 at rehearsal, they were concerned and apprehensive to find that his interpretation of the part was full of new touches. They were even more concerned when he appeared for the performance, for he was flouting tradition in every way—a black wig for the customary red, a clean make-up instead of the usual dirt, and so on. This was no comic villain from the ghetto, but a respectable and prosperous merchant. How would the audience take it?

How they took it is theatre history. The house was very empty, for there had not been much preliminary fuss made about the new actor. But though the spectators were few they knew their theatre and could recognize genius when they saw it. To their eternal credit they recognized it now, though it took an unfamiliar form. After a time one of the actors, Oxberry, listening from the green-room, remarked that he did not know how so few people could make so much noise. There were only two professional critics in the house, but one of them was William Hazlitt, and he not only could recognize genius but knew how to salute it—not with meaningless superlatives, but with a glowing appreciation in which the excitement of the discoverer was not allowed to upset the detachment of the critic. Exactly what Kean did with the part, and exactly how Hazlitt reacted to it, make matter for the next chapter. Here it is enough to chronicle an evening of triumph, which culminated when Kean reached his rooms at Cecil Street and said to his wife the words—so deeply embedded in the Kean tradition that even the careful Hillebrand accepts them without argument —'Mary, you shall ride in your carriage, and Charley shall go to Eton.' It is characteristic both of the man who said those words and the woman to whom he said them that the great moment in their lives should express itself in terms of social advancement.

Social advancement certainly came. Kean's Shylock had made his reputation, and his Richard III on 12 February made his fortune. He became a popular idol, to such an extent that when it was announced that the exertions of acting Richard had made him spit blood, the public constituted itself the guardian of his health and would not hear of his playing the part again till he had himself written to the papers to say that he was perfectly well once more, and that no undue pressure was being put on him by the theatre authorities to play too often. On 26 February Drury Lane doubled his salary and gave him a hundred-guinea bonus; on 12 March, after he had added Hamlet to his list of successes, they raised him to twenty pounds a week, and on 16 July they voted him five subscription shares in the theatre. They could well afford to be generous, for Kean had brought prosperity back to the theatre as if by a miracle. Gifts from patrons flowed in also, as did callers and invitations. Mary Kean's dolefulness was changed to ecstasy, and she not only believed in her husband, but believed that she had always done so.

As for Kean, he had achieved at last his deeply felt ambition to be treated as a gentleman among gentlemen, and at first he took his translation well. It was noticed with approval that his great success had not gone to his head, and that his manners, both in the theatre and in private life, were unassuming. Conscious as he had been all his life, and to a morbid extent, of the defects of his breeding and education, he had tried with pathetic earnestness to get for himself as a man what he had not been given as a boy. During his years as a provincial actor he had worked hard to acquire a smattering of culture, and there are still extant notebooks in which he wrote out phrases in Latin, Greek, and other languages. He had a habit of interlarding his correspondence with these phrases, which he doubtless used with pride, though their effect was to deprive his style of any natural liveliness which it might have had.

Now, however, in company with men of real learning, he found that his very thin veneer of culture was no use to him. On his own subject he could be interesting, but on almost no other had he anything to say. He felt himself hopelessly at a disadvantage, and since it was part of his spoiled-child nature not to be content to play a subordinate part, on the stage or anywhere else, he proclaimed a distaste for high society, and flung himself defiantly into the lowest he could find. Any tavern riff-raff that would drink at his expense and tell him he was a great man was good enough for London's foremost actor. If Garrick and Sarah Siddons had been unpopular in the theatre world because they saved their money, Kean was despised because he flung his away too freely. In his wiser moments he knew that he was endangering his health and his career, but in his more frequent spoiled-child moods he seemed to glory in his bad behaviour.

Perhaps his first visit to the United States in 1820 illustrates better than any other episode in his later career his perverse way of spoiling his own good fortune. For in America he had, and took, a second chance. He went there to find a society prejudiced against him by all the stories it had heard of him, and he broke down that prejudice because his acting was more exciting and his manners more attractive than America had expected. It was a society much more simple and less alarming than the sophisticates of London, and by accepting Kean as a great man and a man of cultivated mind it put him at his ease and took away any temptation to show off. And then, by an ill-judged exhibition of temperament, he turned America against him and threw away all the good that had come to him there. Against advice, he paid a return visit to Boston in the hot weather, not realizing that this was an off-season for American playgoers; and then, offended by the small attendance to see him as Richard III, he refused to go on. Of all his spoiled-child exhibitions this was the one most heavily punished. The American press and public decided that the stories they had heard about him were true, and, worse still, that they had been fooled, and they rounded on him in fury.

The final stages of Kean's story show on the one hand a series of insensate follies amounting at times to something indistinguishable from madness, and on the other a brave battle to keep his position, fought against all kinds of odds. It is easy to condemn him, and there is no doubt that in this procession of the great ones of the English theatre he cuts much the poorest figure. But he had much to contend with in his heredity, and his disintegration began a great deal earlier than has been generally recognized. Playfair disinterred from a lawyer's deed-box a letter to Dr Drury from one J. H. Merivale, dated January 1815, which proves this. The letter is too long to quote at the length which Playfair allows it, but the following are salient passages:

I had hoped to have had some instructions from you to regulate my conduct with respect to poor Kean, having few objects more at heart than to contribute all in my power towards the good work of rescuing him from the imminent dangers which beset him. Evil reports have been crowding in upon us from day to day almost ever since our return in November. . . . At last I took the occasion of our having seen him in Romeo to write him a few lines hinting, in a manner as adroitly combined of flattery and remonstrance as I could well imagine, at the want of proper confidence in his own genius, and ambition of better things, which gave a handle to his enemies and paralysed his own exertions. . . .

On Friday last I called and found Mrs Kean at home, who received me with a hearty shake of the hand, but with a great deal of dejection and apparent embarrassment. 'I have wished much to see you', she said, 'and thank you for your letter', and upon my enquiring how Kean himself took it, she assured me that he was extremely sensible of my friendship, and that nothing but shame could have prevented him from answering it; but that when he received it he was evidently much hurt, would not show her the contents, but merely exclaimed: 'This is all my fault, d——d fool that I am.'

He had never gone so far astray and, it seems, hopelessly astray as about a fortnight since when he went off from town unknown to her, and wrote from Woolwich saying that it was his resolution never to see her or his child again—that she may take all their money but he would find freedom in a foreign country. . . . A day or two later he came back—the fit over—and in a state of contrition at least equal to his former madness. Then came my letter, the next day yours, and with it calls from Whitbread, Grenfell, and Lord Essex, all directed to the same end, and which, she said, had the more confounded him, as he had deceived himself into a previous opinion that his eccentricities were known only to himself and those immediately about him.

From all I could collect it seemed to me very evident that if the poor fellow is to be saved from his friends, now is the time. . . . Yesterday I found him at home and never did I see the gentleman and man of genius more fully combined. . . . He is but an infant in experience; and till you taught him, he never learned to stand upright. No wonder his foot slipped.

In spite of wise and kindly advisers, however, his foot slipped continually. I need not carry the unhappy tale in detail to its close. He died at forty-six, worn out by disease and the excesses of an insanely ill-regulated life. But he had established his place in history. He lived in a period when the London public was extremely expert in its appreciation of the player's art, and when that expertness found expression in criticism of acting more exact, elaborate, and perceptive than had been attempted before or has been achieved since. The men who wrote that criticism knew great acting when they saw it; and they saw it in Edmund Kean.

Chapter 9

SHAKESPEARE LIT BY LIGHTNING

THE DRAMA CRITICS OF TO-DAY HAVE ALMOST LOST THE ART OF detailed examination of acting, which was carried to its highest pitch of excellence by their predecessors a century ago. They have been forced to lose it by a variety of circumstances. It may sound ungracious in me to say that men like Hazlitt, Lamb, and Leigh Hunt, the pioneers of drama criticism as we know it to-day, wrote brilliantly about acting because it was all they had to write about, but it is true all the same. In their day the monopoly of the Patent Theatres still held, and only at those great theatres were the plays put on worthy of critical attention; and the vast majority of these plays were classics and near-classics so familiar to the public that they not only could, but must, be taken for granted. The playgoers' chief interest lay not in the plays themselves, but in the actors' interpretation of the leading parts, and the critics' first concern was to assess the work of a new performer, to notice if and where and how effectively he departed from established tradition, and to compare his interpretation with those of his rivals. The appearance of an occasional new play was certainly an event, but here again the interest lay less in the merit of the play itself than in the novelty of seeing favourite performers in unfamiliar characters. The drama critic of those early days was, in fact, in precisely the same position as the modern music critic at the opera.

When the monopoly was broken and the 'legitimate' theatres multiplied, the demand for new plays increased greatly and the dramatist, assuming a new importance, established a claim on the critic's attention which could only be honoured at the actor's expense. A similar change took place in the attitude of the public. Although the average playgoer still went to the theatre to see the actors rather than the play—and has continued to do so to this day—he soon came to expect a new play to be provided each time the actor appeared, and was not prepared to go to see even the most popular actor unless critical opinion assured him that the play was worth while.

The critics of the late Victorian age, having at their disposal a great deal of newspaper space, were able to deal with this situation. Writing for newspapers with small circulations which did not go to press until the early hours of the morning, they had not only space but time at their disposal. Having analysed a new play at great length, they were still able to devote half a column or more of close print to the actors' work. Increase of circulation, making necessary a progressively earlier hour of publication, brought those spacious days to an end. Rapid new methods of communication, bringing news from the four corners of the world, made editors more chary of their space. Even before the last war and its aftermath brought paper restrictions, newspaper criticisms were growing shorter and the space devoted to acting proportionately small. The Hazlitt of to-day, if he exists, must make his effects not by carefully observed detail exactly rendered, but by quick bold impressionistic strokes and happy phrases. Even when he gets the chance to write at length he cannot go into detail as the old masters did. His observation and his memory have been trained in a different way.

Kean was in many ways a most unfortunate man but he was lucky in his period. Because he lived just when he did posterity knows him better than it knows any other great player of the past with the possible exception of Irving. A happy phrase has certainly played its part in perpetuating his fame, for Coleridge's remark that to watch Kean act was like reading Shakespeare by flashes of lightning is an inspired piece of description, which itself lights up its subject like any lightning-flash. But even if Coleridge had never said it, Hazlitt and his contemporary critics fill in for us the picture of a stormy, fitful, but unmistakable genius. Not all these critics accepted Kean as a genius, however. Those who held that the Kemble way of playing tragedy was the only way—and they included *The Times* critic—praised Kean faintly or were loud in denunciation. But they were also exact in observation and objective in description, so that even from their denunciations we can add details to the picture of Kean that forms in our minds as we read; and the very bitterness with which they defended their citadel shows how dangerous they thought its assailant. Hazlitt's first notice in *The Morning Chronicle* must have sounded a challenge which warned all the defenders to man the walls, for Hazlitt did not care for Kemble's cold correctitude, and he was delighted to celebrate the arrival of this so different player, saying straight out

that for voice, eye, action, and expression no actor had come out
for many years at all equal to him:

In giving effect to the conflict of passions arising out of the contrast of situation,
in varied vehemence of declamation, in keenness of sarcasm, in the rapidity of
his transitions from one tone and feeling to another, in propriety and novelty
of action, presenting a series of striking pictures, and giving perpetually fresh
shocks of delight and surprise—it would be difficult to single out a competitor.

This was unequivocal enough, but next day Hazlitt went even
further, proclaiming that Kean's performance had been 'distinguished by characteristics which fix him at once in the first rank
of his profession'.

This brought in some of the critics who had not been at the first
performance, and one of them, in *The Examiner*, went to greater
lengths than Hazlitt. After admitting that Kean had an insignificant figure and a voice 'somewhat between an apoplexy and a
cold', he went on to say that in spite of these defects:

There was an animating soul distinguishable in all he said and did which at
once gave a high interest to his performance, and excited those emotions which
are always felt at the presence of genius—that is, at the union of great powers
with a fine sensibility. It was this that gave fire to his eye, energy to his tones,
and such a variety and expressiveness to all his gestures, that one might almost
say 'his body thought'.

After this the cool admission of *The Times* that except for Kemble
(of course) and Cooke it had not seen a better Shylock seems as
grudging as no doubt the writer of the notice intended.

With the production of *Richard III*, and the beginning of Kean's
real triumph, *The Examiner* is more exuberant than ever:

We cannot recall any performance—the very first exhibitions of Mrs Siddons
not excepted—which was so calculated to delight an audience and to impress
it with veneration for the talents of an actor. . . . We never felt stronger emotions, more overpowering sensations, than were kindled by the novel sublimity
of this catastrophe [namely, the death scene].

Hazlitt had himself more firmly under control, but is all the
more impressive for that:

It is possible to form a higher conception of this character (we do not mean from
seeing other actors, but from reading Shakespeare) than that given by this very
admirable tragedian; but we cannot imagine any character represented with
greater distinction and precision, more perfectly articulated in every part. . . .
If Mr Kean does not completely succeed in concentrating all the lines of the
character, as drawn by Shakespeare, he gives an animation, vigour, and relief

to the part, which we have never seen surpassed. . . . He filled every part of the stage.

In the wooing of Anne 'he seemed, like the first tempter, to approach his prey, certain of the event, and as if success had smoothed the way before him'; while in the death scene:

He fought like one drunk with wounds; and the attitude in which he stands with his hands stretched out, after his sword is taken from him, had a preternatural and terrific grandeur, as if his will could not be disarmed, and the very phantoms of his despair had power to kill.

The Morning Post finds this death scene 'greatness itself', calls his exit into his tent 'one of the finest pieces of acting we have ever beheld, or perhaps that the stage has ever known', and also picks out for special praise the scene where Richard is taunted by the little Duke of York:

A finer picture of stifled rage, and affected composure, can hardly be conceived. This is not marked by a grim aside, nor is it accompanied by any theatrical flourish. It is done without effort, and its delicacy constitutes its strength.

This time *The Times* is loftily patronizing:

He is evidently a player of no ordinary cast, and as from his youth he will not want time for improvement, he is in all probability destined to shine in his profession. . . . He excelled in the cutting and the sarcastic; but he was not equally fortunate in the loftier darings of the heroic.

Yet even this critic makes one deeply significant remark—he praises Kean for being himself and imitating nobody. And this opinion is elaborated by a knowledgeable playgoer, Sir George Beaumont, in a passage quoted by Hillebrand from the diary of Farington the painter:

No actor since Garrick exhibited so much genuine feeling of nature. At times he appears to be Richard himself. He never can have dignity or grace, his person is too diminutive, but he is a true natural actor, and wholly free from the measured and artificial practice of the Kemble school.

This impression of naturalness is deepened by a description which the actor George Vandenhoff gives of Kean's playing in the great speech where Shylock elaborates the reasons for his hatred of Antonio. I give this passage with some reserve, for Vandenhoff was a child when Kean died, and must have had the account by hearsay from his father—another actor. It rings true, but it is at second hand for all that:

This was always the cue for the most intense applause: it was the natural simplicity with which he gave it, the sort of patient appeal his voice seemed to make to your sympathy against undeserved oppression, that touched the heart and the intellect at once. He hurried you on through the catalogue of Antonio's atrocities and unprovoked injuries to him, enforcing them with a strong accentuation, and a high pitch of voice; and when he had reached the climax, he came down by a sudden transition to a gentle suffering tone of simple representation of his oppressor's manifest unreason and injustice, in the words: 'I am a *Jew*!' and the effect was instantaneous.

This effect of naturalness seems at first sight very much the same as that which Mrs Siddons produced on her audiences in the early part of her career. But if the effect was similar, the method by which it was produced was altogether different. We have seen Mrs Siddons working herself up so that she could take the stage with her emotions already well ablaze; but Kean, if we are to believe both his own remark that he never felt any emotion on the stage except when he was acting with a pretty woman, and the many pieces of testimony from others, was a living proof that art is emotion remembered in tranquillity. It was on the long, lonely walks of his strolling-player days that he identified himself with his characters and felt their passions. On the stage he was strictly an interpretative artist, with the creative period quite at an end, as was shown by the recorded fact that his performances never varied from night to night—except, of course, in that subtle adaptation of tempo to the reactions of each individual audience which is an essential part of every professional player's equipment. It is odd to reflect that Sarah Siddons, according to tradition the very type of correctitude and contrivance, was in fact a creature of impulse; while Kean, by common report dependent on divine but intermittent inspiration, never made an effect not precisely calculated beforehand.

Sometimes he altered his original conception, not always for the better. At such times the critics were ready for him. Comparison between one performer and another in the same part was their regular avocation, and comparison between an actor and his own worse self was only another exercise of the same faculty. Here, for example, is Hazlitt, writing in *The Champion* on 9 October 1814, when Kean had returned to Drury Lane after his first visit to Dublin, and had opened with *Richard III*.

We do not think Mr Kean at all improved by his Irish expedition. . . . His pauses are twice as long as they were, and the rapidity with which he hurries over other parts of the dialogue is twice as great as it was. In both these points his style of acting always bordered on the very verge of extravagance; and we suspect it has at present passed the line. . . The quickness of familiar utterance with which Mr Kean pronounced the anticipated doom of Stanley, 'Chop off his head', was quite ludicrous. . . . He frequently varied the execution of many of his most striking conceptions, and the attempt in general failed, as it naturally must do. . . . We object particularly to his varying the original action in the dying scene. He at first held out his hands in a way which can only be conceived by those who saw him—in motionless despair—or as if there was some preter-natural power in the mere manifestation of his will; he now actually fights with his doubled fists, after his sword is taken from him, like some helpless infant.

(It may be remarked here in parenthesis that while we can sympa-thize with Hazlitt's indignation at seeing so drastic an alteration made in the very stroke of acting which he had singled out for special praise at his first view of Kean's Richard, and while a comparison of his two descriptions makes us agree with him that the change was for the worse, still we must salute Kean's courage and origin-ality. Most actors would have been content, after Hazlitt's tribute, to stereotype that particular passage. Kean took the tribute as a challenge to try to improve even on his excellences, and that he failed ought not to be counted against him.)

Hazlitt proceeds:

We really think that Mr Kean was in a great many instances either too familiar, too emphatic, or too energetic. In the latter scenes, perhaps, his energy could not be too great; but he gave the energy of action alone. He merely gesticulated, or at best vociferated the part. His articulation totally failed him.

The critic then says he blames the managers for making Kean play the same parts over and over again instead of allowing him to vary his repertoire; and we are left speculating with interest as to what he may be saying now if, from the astral plane, he con-templates the modern long-run system. Then he goes on:

Ill as we conceive the London managers have treated him, the London audiences have treated him well; and we wish Mr Kean, for some years at least, to stick to them. . . After he has got through the season here well we see no reason why he should make himself hoarse with performing Hamlet at twelve o'clock and Richard at six, at Kidderminster. . . To a man of genius, leisure is the first of benefits as well as of luxuries.

It would have been well for Kean if he had been of a nature well enough balanced to take this sage advice. He bitterly despised the country audiences which had been incapable of appreciating his acting when he was unknown, but were tumbling over one another to see exactly the same performances now that they had received the London *imprimatur*. It did him no good spiritually to act to them, and it tired him out physically. But it filled his pockets—he could command as much as fifty pounds a night for appearing at a big provincial theatre—and money was the symbol of success. He continued to accept engagements in the country, even on occasion breaking faith with the Drury Lane public to which, as Hazlitt clearly saw, he owed his position.

I doubt if I could find in all theatrical history an event that goes farther than the rise of Kean to justify my growing belief that no actor can be great unless and until he finds an audience worthy of him. None of the players whose careers have been outlined in previous chapters gives us much evidence on this point. We have no real record of Burbage's or Betterton's beginnings. Garrick brought off the miracle, personal to himself, of stepping straight to the head of his profession without any previous experience to speak of. Mrs Siddons had her first chance at Drury Lane before she was equal to the ordeal. Kean, on the other hand, came to London with his technical equipment fully under control; the performances which Hazlitt acclaimed, and which excited the theatre-wise and responsive London audiences to frenzy, were identical in form with the performances he had been giving to thin, apathetic houses at Dorchester when Arnold went down to see him there. In a certain absolute sense, then, Kean was a 'great' actor before he came to Drury Lane. And yet what Arnold saw at Dorchester was not great acting, simply because great acting needs not merely recognition but actual co-operation from an audience, and the Dorchester audience was not able to rise to the occasion.

Those audiences in Dorchester—and all the other provincial audiences in Guernsey, or Exeter, or Barnstaple, before which Kean was playing just before his translation—failed to play their part not out of inborn crassness but from inbred prejudice, not from stupidity but from ignorance. They knew, or thought they knew, when they came to the theatre, that tragedy could properly be acted only in measured tones of grandeur by big impressive men and statuesque women. They knew, or thought they knew, that tragic parts acted with vehemence by a little man, with nothing impressive about him except a pair of flashing black eyes, amounted to something very like a contradiction in terms. No doubt the little man was doing his best—perhaps doing very well considering his physical handicaps—but he was obviously miscast, and therefore could not really be any good. Any audience which comes to the theatre in such a frame of mind puts up a sort of subconscious passive resistance against which an actor's best efforts may hurl themselves in vain. The actor, finding opposition where he needs co-operation, either gives in and falls at once below his best, or spends himself in a vain attempt to break down the audience's prejudice against him. In neither case is he able to give a great performance, however capable of greatness he may be in the absolute sense.

That Kean was perfectly conscious of this many stories show. Two of them come to us in his own words. One night he heard that Lord Cork, who was supposed to be something of a judge of acting, was coming to see him play, and bringing his family. From the actor's point of view the occasion was a miserable failure, and his indignation was great. 'Whilst I was playing the finest parts of Othello in my best style, my Lord Cork's children were playing at hot cockles in front of the box and Lord and Lady Cork laughing at them.' This disappointment was all the greater because the one way in which he could keep his confidence in himself alive was to find a responsive playgoer somewhere in the audience—for example, Dr Drury at Exeter—and play for him alone. That was what happened when Arnold came to Dorchester; Kean was playing Octavian in Colman's *The Mountaineers* to a small and unrewarding audience when he noticed a stranger in a box who, like Lord Cork, did not look like a provincial and, unlike Lord Cork, was following Kean's performance with close attention. Luckily for him, his response to this small degree of encouragement was immediate enough and strong enough to convince Arnold that the little man was worth an extended London trial. But it is not to be thought that Kean touched greatness on this night.

Acting does not exist at all until it finds an audience of some kind; great acting cannot exist at all until it finds an audience of the right kind. Kean could not give a great performance until he was helped to it by an audience ready to judge by what it felt, and not by what it thought it ought to feel. Some potentially great actors never find such an audience, and never touch greatness in consequence; some find such audiences now and again, and become great players on a particular occasion or even for the run of a particular play. Either of these fates might have been Kean's, but he was lucky enough to find an audience ready and able to follow him to the heights as often as he was able to lead them there. Well might Hazlitt say that the London audiences 'had treated him well'.

As I have said, Kean was apt in later years to be deeply scornful of the provincial audiences which, having neglected him when he was unknown, flocked to see him, wept their eyes out over him, and praised him to the skies once he had made a big reputation. If he had been capable of thinking the matter out dispassionately he might have abated his scorn. The truth is that when the provincial playgoers saw Kean after his London triumphs they were really looking at him for the first time. The things which they had thought they knew about acting had turned out, mysteriously but un-mistakably, not to be knowledge. It appeared after all that the idea of tragedy being acted by small vehement men was not in-herently absurd. Prejudice vanished, and unconscious passive re-sistance went with it automatically. For the first time these play-goers were able to subject themselves to the emotional impact of Kean's playing, and their surrender to it was not, as Kean thought, the result of a snobbish desire to be in the swim, but a genuine tribute to his powers. Kean was in fact blaming the provinces for being provincial. That is to say, he was demanding of compara-tively small, remote communities, from which most of the brighter spirits in every walk of life had drifted to London to seek their fortunes, that they should display a startling independence of judge-ment. Even to-day, when the elimination of distance and the spread of education enables the provincial cities to challenge London's dictatorship in the other arts, we find the most forward-looking theatrical managers in those cities complaining that they can only with difficulty persuade audiences to accept anything without Lon-don's hallmark. Kean, then, was being neither logical nor fair when he spoke with scorn of his rapturous audiences outside London; but perhaps neither logic nor justice was to be expected of him, since he had been deeply hurt.

How great was his impact upon audiences that were receptive to his methods is best seen from the fact that he made his greatest effects in the part of Sir Giles Overreach, the villain of Philip Massinger's play, *A New Way to Pay Old Debts*. This play ranks as one of the most remarkable products of the Jacobean theatre, that turgid and gloomy period of writing which is so magnificent to read and so difficult (but sometimes rewarding) to stage. Over-reach is not often seen on the stage, because he is a character of such unrelenting malignancy that in the hands of any but the most powerful of actors he becomes ridiculous. It is a characteristic of such parts that they either show the actor off or show him up; and theatrical history records few actors who have dared to tackle

Overreach, and fewer still who have emerged successful from the encounter. Not for seventy years has the part been played in the West End, and except for a production at the Old Vic in 1922, when Robert Atkins played the part and was received with respect, the play has not had an important revival within living memory. Yet Kean's power was such that he could take even this tremendous personage in his stride, so that a character which would have seemed incredible and melodramatic was reduced to proportions which, though horrifying, were human. In other words, Overreach can be acted without absurdity only by a man who can give the part everything that it calls for and still suggest that he is playing within himself and could, if necessary, release still further reserves of power.

Hillebrand's account of Kean's acting in the part, carefully collected from various sources, shows clearly enough—even though the biographer's customary caution leads him into understatement —that the suggestion of latent power was so great as to be actually terrifying:

His great moments came in the final scene, where Overreach, cornered and exposed, lashes out in ungoverned fury at his pursuers, goes mad in fact from his own rage, foams, curses, and falls into a catalepsy. Here Kean was transcendent; no scene of a similar nature that he had previously exhibited came anywhere near it. The pit rose bellowing. Lord Byron, as is well known, fell over in a convulsion, and, what is more remarkable, even the actors were affected by it. We may discount the over-coloured picture imagined by Hawkins, of Mrs Glover fainting, Mrs Horn breaking into hysterical tears, and Munden, stiffened with terror, dragged off the stage by his armpits. But there is sufficient testimony to the effect that the actors were visibly astonished and that Mrs Glover had suddenly to find a chair. This in itself is sufficiently impressive.

The understatement lies in the fact that almost immediately after this passage Hillebrand quotes a letter from Mary Kean's sister, Susan Chambers, to a friend in Ireland, in which she says: 'To see him in the last act I think you never would get over it. Mrs Glover got into strong hysterics and several ladies fainted.' As Hillebrand brings forward no reason why the writer of this letter should have the evidence of her eyes doubted, we are free to believe that Mrs Glover experienced an emotion a good deal more cataclysmic than a sudden desire to sit down. Hazlitt found the conclusion of the play 'quite overwhelming', could find not a single fault, and said that while he had seen others in the part, 'superior in the look and costume, in hardened, clownish, rustic insensibility', no one had equalled Kean in the soul and spirit. This was a direct reference to Kemble, in whose repertoire Overreach had been since 1783; and Kemble was unwise enough to accept the challenge and play the part again. The result was a disaster for Kemble, and Hazlitt recorded it as such, sadly but without partiality, saying that he had hardly ever experienced any more painful feeling than when 'the sanguine plaudits of Mr Kemble's friends' were drowned by a volley of hisses from the pit.

That this part, played with such consummate force, should have been the high peak of Kean's achievements, seems entirely credible when we read a very able American summing-up of the actor's faults and virtues, made at his second visit to the United States in 1821, and quoted by Hillebrand. The writer is an unidentified Philadelphian journalist who wrote under the pseudonym of 'Betterton':

He is eminently successful in situations which admit of intense fire and vivacity of action, inarticulate passion, or rapid alterations of countenance and tone. Sudden and strong vicissitudes of feeling are admirably portrayed in the movements of his features. His eye conveys the most opposite meaning and sensation with singular quickness of transition and versatility of eloquence.

These are great virtues, but they carry their own inherent dangers with them:

His excellences are perpetually passing into extremes or degenerating into defects. He is always in his happiest exhibitions of art, and most brilliant flashes of genius, on the verge of extravagance. . . . His studied play of physiognomy borders on grimace; his animation of manner becomes incoherent bustle; what is spirited savours of turbulence; what is passionate of frenzy. He obviously relies more on mechanical resources than on his general mental preparation and powers, or his fervour of feeling and thorough possession of his part. He is called a natural player, but his style of acting is highly artificial and technical; it is uniformly elaborate, systematic and ambitious. Nothing is left to the inspiration of the moment.

One suspects from this account that 'Betterton', for all his objectivity, was not temperamentally sympathetic to the kind of acting he is describing. He is no less valuable a witness for that; and he proves one thing clearly—that in his art Kean could keep his wildness under that iron control which in his life he was never able to achieve.

Chapter 10

THE MAGNIFICENCE OF IRVING

EDMUND KEAN DIED IN 1833, AND HIS PLACE AT THE HEAD OF his profession was taken and held for many years by a very different man, William Charles Macready, son of that Macready whom we have seen turning pale at Sarah Siddons's most spectacular death scene. That Macready at his best was a very fine actor indeed is not to be doubted, or that he had in him the potentiality of greatness. His claim to take the next place in our procession of the great ones must not be dismissed unheard; yet it cannot, I think, be admitted. He was a man at odds with himself and with the world, as his diaries show. He missed greatness because he could not achieve singleness of mind. I shall return to him later when the procession has passed; but meanwhile Kean's true successor makes his belated approach, and demands our attention.

It was about half a century after Kean's death that the following sympathetic and understanding words paid tribute to his memory:

The road to success lies through many a thorny course, across many a dreary stretch of desert land, over many an obstacle, from which the fainting heart is often tempted to turn back. But hope, and a sense of power within, which no discouragement can subdue, inspire the struggling artist still to continue the conflict, till at last courage and perseverance meet with their just reward, and success comes. The only feeling then to which the triumphant artist may be tempted is one of good-natured contempt for those who are so ready to applaud those merits which, in the past, they were too blind to recognize.

The words, all but one, were true of Kean; for it is greatly to be doubted whether his contempt for the provincial audiences who had failed to recognize his merits could ever have been called 'good-natured'. But the words were completely true of the man who wrote them; for he was Henry Irving.

Kean and Irving had this in common, that they had to face more than their fair share of frustration and disappointment at the outset of their careers, and that their success, even when won, was maintained in the face of much hostile criticism. They also had in common certain characteristics in their methods of acting, as will

119

appear in due course. In other ways, and particularly in the conduct of their lives off the stage, they were as unlike as it is possible
for two men to be. Kean had at the core of his being a deep unease
which made of him in the end a social outcast; Irving had a calm
certainty of his right to respect which enabled him not only to win
for himself a position in society which no actor had held before
him, but to rid his calling, finally and for ever, of that stigma of
roguery and vagabondage of which it had still not ridded itself.
When the Garrick Club was founded in 1831, only seven years
before Irving's birth, its constitution laid down that it was intended to be a place 'where actors and men of education and refinement might meet on equal terms'. At that time such words
could still be written seriously and accepted unquestioningly; and
the fact that they have now become a joke is due chiefly to Irving.
Half a century after the Garrick's foundation, when Irving as
accepted leader of the English theatre had just enlarged the
Lyceum Theatre, W. S. Gilbert was able to make his Lord Chan-
cellor in *Iolanthe* mention the actor's calling in very different
terms:

> In other professions in which men engage,
>   Said I to myself, said I,
> The army, the navy, the church, or the stage,
>   Said I to myself, said I,
> Professional licence, if carried too far,
> Your chance of promotion will certainly mar,
> And I fancy the rule might apply to the bar,
>   Said I to myself, said I.

You may object that this means little—that Gilbert was availing
himself of a convenient rhyme, or even taking an opportunity to
give the stage a veneer of respectability that it did not yet possess.
The fact remains that in 1882 Gilbert was able to mention the
stage in a list of the honourable professions without outraging public
sentiment, and that Queen Victoria signified her agreement with
this idea in 1895 when she conferred on Henry Irving the first
knighthood ever given to an actor. Even Irving himself did not
realize what a difference he had made, for Gordon Craig heard
him say, 'They'll knight no other actors after me.' He could not
foresee that from his time onward 'men of education and refinement' would more and more turn to the theatre as a place in
which to find not merely aesthetic delight but their lives' work.

Possibly for the reason that he made the theatre seem more important than ever before, or possibly because he lived in an age

which was apt to make portentous figures of its great men, there is a vast Irving literature. In the case of Burbage and Betterton I had to make excuse because there was too little material to serve my special purpose in this book; but concerning Irving there is altogether too much. There are two big biographies, by Bram Stoker and by Austin Brereton, and there is a mass of incidental biographical writing and critical controversy. Into none of this do I propose to delve for more than a few straightforward facts, for to do so would be a digression, and an unnecessary digression at that. Only three questions about Irving concern me—what kind of a man was he, what kind of an actor was he, and what effect did he and his audiences have upon one another? These questions are all dealt with in a special way by Gordon Craig in his book *Henry Irving*, and because of that I can rely on Craig and leave the other authors on their crowded shelf.

Not that Craig's book is reliable in any scientifically historical sense. It is discursive, untidy, and incomplete, considered as biography. It even leaves you in some doubt about its facts, for when Irving himself gives a date for some event and his biographers show by documentary proof that another date is correct, Craig blandly sticks to Irving's version, saying that he is not going to give support to any idea that his old master can be, like other mortals, fallible. For all that, it is a book of very great value. It is an impression of one great artist by another, and therefore a book quite different in kind from any other on which I have so far been able to draw. For half a dozen reasons, Craig is the ideal man to be the interpreter of Irving. He has intimate knowledge, because he was both the son of Irving's leading lady Ellen Terry, and an actor in the Lyceum company. He has freedom from any suspicion of professional jealousy of Irving, because he did not remain an actor long. He has sympathetic understanding, because the theatre is in his blood, and by the theatre his own reputation was made. He has the deep admiration of the pupil for the master, and yet the detachment to realize that his own work of bringing new ideas to the theatre became possible only when he threw off that master's influence. In this book, therefore, if anywhere, the essential Irving is to be found, and there I shall search for him. But first, some facts.

Irving was not the actor's original name. He was born in Somerset in 1838, the son of a small shopkeeper, and he was baptized John Henry Brodribb. His mother, whose maiden name was Mary Behenna, was of Cornish peasant stock, and it was with a sister of hers in Cornwall that the boy spent his early years. Here he was brought up in strict piety with no formal education, and he had no proper schooling till he rejoined his parents in London at the age of eleven and was sent to the City Commercial School in George Yard, the headmaster of which had the menacing name of Doctor Pinches. Here, it is said, he acted in school plays and got his first glimpse of the theatre; it was a case of love at first sight, and two years later, when he had left school and had gone to work in an office, he took his first step towards becoming an actor. He joined the City Elocution Class under Henry Thomas, and quickly won some reputation as a reciter who always knew his lines. A visit to Sadler's Wells Theatre, where he saw Samuel Phelps as Hamlet, strengthened his ambition, and it was characteristic of his thoroughness that in subsequent visits to Phelps's theatre he read and carefully studied the plays beforehand. He met a member of Phelps's company named William Hoskins, who introduced him to Phelps and got him the offer of a job at Sadler's Wells. Characteristically again, the boy refused, having made up his mind that he must start in the provinces. He took lessons from Hoskins in the mornings before starting for his office, and then, in 1856 at the age of eighteen, he went to Sunderland with a letter in his pocket from Hoskins to the manager of the theatre there, one E. D. Davies.

From the very first he was unusual. He had a gentlemanly air which told in his favour, but the mannerisms which were to be the subject of acid comment all through his professional career were already part of his style, and Craig quotes a Sunderland journalist who urged him, after his first appearance, 'to take the first steamer back to his comfortable home, and to abandon all hope of becoming an actor'. Instead, the young man—his name was Henry Irving now and henceforward—went on to Edinburgh, stayed there for over two years, and played, according to Brereton, 429 parts in that time. This astonishing apprenticeship brought him his second London offer, and he accepted an engagement at the Princess's Theatre. However, he resigned it again on finding that he was to be given only very small parts, and went to Dublin instead with a promise that he should play Florizel and Laertes.

Here a horrible experience awaited him. There was a feeling among the Dublin public, always excitable and ready to take sides in a quarrel, that the actor whom Irving was replacing had been wrongfully dismissed. Accordingly, for a number of weeks variously estimated at from three to six, the audience vented its anger on the innocent usurper. Here is Irving's own account:

There was I standing aghast, ignorant of having given any cause of offence, and in front of me a raging Irish audience, shouting, gesticulating, swearing volubly, and in various forms indicating their disapproval of my appearance. Night after night, I had to fight through my part in the teeth of a house whose entire energies seemed to be concentrated in a personal antipathy to myself.

He fought through this, and when at last the rioters felt that their protest had been duly lodged, he won approval; but the ordeal was a fierce one for a sensitive artist. Craig suggests that he gained strength from it, and also makes the likely conjecture that it was here he learnt his aloof attitude towards praise and censure alike, and his way of not accepting applause but only enduring it.

After this came five years in Manchester under Charles Calvert —five years of steady but slow progress, in which he gradually asserted his right to be given the most important parts. Towards the end of this engagement he played Hamlet, but was held not to have enough physical or vocal power for a part so exacting, and this may have been the reason why in 1865 he refused yet another invitation to come to London, this time to join Fechter's company at the Lyceum. However, it is certain that about this time he began to feel that his novitiate was over, because in 1866 he accepted an invitation to create the part of Rawdon Scudamore in Dion Boucicault's *Hunted Down*, on condition that he should have the part in London if the play succeeded. It did succeed, and in October Irving joined Miss Herbert's company at the St James's Theatre. In November the Boucicault play was presented and Irving, playing his original part, had favourable notices. In February of the following year he did well in a revival of *The Road to Ruin*, and might consider himself reasonably firmly established as a London actor. Towards the end of that year he played Petruchio at the Queen's Theatre; and though the performance added nothing to his reputation it deserves mention even in the briefest epitome of his career, for Katharine was played by Ellen Terry, and this was the first time these two famous partners acted together.

Two more years went by before Irving scored a real personal success, which he did as Digby Grant in James Albery's *The Two Roses* at the Vaudeville in June 1870. Then, in 1871, unheralded and unexpected, came the triumph towards which he had been working so long and devotedly. He had been engaged by an American manager, Colonel Bateman, who had taken the Lyceum Theatre chiefly in order to launch his young daughter, Isabel Bateman, on her career. Bateman's first two productions failed ignominiously and he was about to throw his hand in when Irving persuaded him somehow, against his better judgement, to put into rehearsal a dramatization by Leopold Lewis of a French story called *Le Juif Polonais*. Irving saw in the leading part something for himself, but nobody else had any hope for the play at all, and while the rehearsals were going on another version of the same original story was produced at a theatre in Marylebone, and failed. A feeling of utter depression settled down on the Lyceum; and in this atmosphere, on 25 November 1871, Irving appeared in *The Bells* and stepped to the head of his profession.

Craig calls this play Irving's masterpiece, with perfect accuracy because he is using the word in its proper sense not as meaning an artist's best work but the work by which his claim to be a master of his craft is first established. *The Bells* is not a great play, but of its kind it is a good one, and a good test of a tragedian. To Irving it was something more than that, a vehicle for his own personal and particular ability. The part of Mathias served Irving as the part of Isabella served Mrs Siddons, as something theatrically effective which would show London that a new player of the first rank had come to town. Just as London had had to wait some years till Mrs Siddons showed it her full power as Lady Macbeth, so it had to wait till 1874 for Irving to prove himself, by his Hamlet, supreme among living actors. Meanwhile in *The Bells* he saved the fortunes of the Lyceum and established his own. What he did with this part to make it peculiarly his, and how he did it, will be discussed in the next chapter. Here let the fact be enough.

In 1875 Bateman died, leaving the management of the theatre to his wife. But by this time, to the playgoing public, the name associated with the Lyceum was no longer Bateman's but Irving's. Irving had too firm an idea of what he wanted to do to work much longer under any management but his own. Soon it was clear that Mrs Bateman must either resign the theatre to Irving or continue to run it without him; and the second alternative being by now unthinkable, she chose the first. In 1878 Irving became manager of the Lyceum and invited Ellen Terry to join him as his leading lady. He enlarged and improved the theatre, and ruled it—and from it, theatrical London—like a king. The last word is chosen with deliberation, for there was something royal about Irving's position at the Lyceum. His lavish hospitality, for instance, was not like the extravagance of a spendthrift, nor had it the careless 'easy-come-easy-go' atmosphere in which too many successful players have felt compelled to squander their fortunes. It had something more like the magnificence of a court in which, for official reasons, a higher standard of entertainment must be kept up than the state of its exchequer can justify. Irving was a link between the theatre and the great world in a way never before known, even in Garrick's day. At a period when high society was no less exclusive and people in general much more respectable than ever before, the breaking down of the old prejudice against stage-players was more than remarkable—it was miraculous. Doubtless it was in some way a sign of the times. The high moral and social standard set by the Kembles and carried on by men like Macready must have had its effect. Yet we know from his own writings how deeply Macready—still alive when Irving first came to the Lyceum—resented the cold-shouldering which actors of education and refinement like himself still had to bear from neighbours in the country. Irving may have found the soil partly prepared for him, but it was he who sowed the seed and reaped the harvest, and an astonishingly swift harvest too. Only twelve years after his first emergence from the ranks of ordinary London actors, and only five after he became his own manager, in 1883 that is, he was approached about the possibility of his being offered a knighthood. He refused it then, seeing in it only a personal tribute of a kind which caused him no particular gratification. Twelve years later he accepted, realizing that the offer was not simply an individual compliment but a public and explicit repudiation of the idea that an actor, however worthy a citizen in himself, must always rank officially below the salt. More gratifying, because more directly a tribute to the art which he served, was the invitation in the same year (1895) to speak at the Royal Academy banquet. He was the first actor to be invited to do this, and as a corollary to the invitation the drama was for the first time included in the list of arts to be honoured with a toast.

Irving's character and career stand out in contrast with those of the other great figures of our stage in their unhurried pace and solid achievement. Garrick and Sarah Siddons and Kean were all in their twenties when they conquered London; Irving was thirty-five. They were eager to conquer London at the first assault, and to launch that assault at the earliest moment; he was content to collect his forces at leisure before attacking. Craig accounts for this quality of patience by his farming ancestry, and the theory is too attractive not to be adopted. But with that patience went the relentless concentration of genius.

Craig brings this side of Irving out very clearly.

He was a selfish man [he says bluntly] and it is ridiculous to try to picture him as thinking over-considerately of others, or of the other arts. . . . Irving was a selfish man without a jot of self-interest. He was without consideration for anybody else, never spared himself, and would never unprovoked hurt anyone. He had a failing (I suppose it must be called a weakness) and that was that he too often credited others with his own powers of endurance and self-criticism. He had no toleration for any signs of feebleness in himself, and he credited us all with a like capacity for self-discipline.

This passage, among others, was given serial publication in *The Times*, and an old friend of Craig's objected to the word 'selfish' as being likely to cause misunderstanding. In the published book, therefore, Craig elucidates in a footnote:

I mean this—that Irving in his theatre was what Napoleon was in the midst of his army. Irving was sole ruler of the theatre of England from 1871 till his death. No ruler is either fool enough or cruel enough to be an altruist. What he cares for most—cares solely for—is the thing over which he has come to rule. Irving's kindness was well-known, his patience was astounding; but patient and kind as he was to us all, he thought for himself and of himself: never spared himself—spared us very often—and yet more often spared no one.

His will was all that mattered in the Lyceum Theatre. The man who wills the rest of mankind to do as he wishes is a selfish man. . . . So the word 'selfish' must stand. . . . So devoted was Irving to our stage that he really was innocently selfish. My mother often used to say, with a lovely twinkle in her eyes: 'Yes, yes—were I to be run over by a steam-roller to-morrow, Henry would be deeply grieved; would say quietly: "What a pity!"—and would add, after two moments' reflection: "Who is there—er—to go on for her to-night?" ' She knew he was selfish for our British Theatre's sake—that he placed the stage above the ground, as a priest does his church, and that whether he dropped dead or she . . . the play must go on.

It is in the light of this furious concentration upon one thing in life, then, that all Irving's qualities, and no less his failings, should be judged. For example, it is not denied by any of his admirers that in spite of his kindness of heart he was a terrifying personage, or that in spite of his generous hospitality he made a formidable figure at the head of a table, whether that table was his own at the Lyceum, or the long one in the centre of the dining-room at the Garrick Club. He presided there almost as a matter of right after a London performance; Guy Boas, in his book on the Club, says that even now to look at the seat at the head of that table is to fancy that at any moment Irving may rise again, like Banquo, to push whosoever sits there from his stool. Boas goes on:

What were the sensations of his more timid contemporaries, who lined the sides of the table in his presence, it is not easy to conjecture. 'I regret, sir,' Irving was wont to remark to anyone who rose from the table before him, 'that you are fatigued by our company.' Many an exhausted member, we are told, remained in his place long after his appropriate bedtime rather than incur that majestic rebuke. And Irving was no early sleeper. About eleven forty-five, records G.P. Bancroft, the theatres being over, 'the door of the Garrick dining-room would open, and Irving with two or three guests would come in fresh from his work and ready for a late night. He was a demon for sitting up in his day clothes, with the invariable black spats in winter-time. He would stroll quite unselfconsciously to the desk to order his haddock or kidneys, but I can feel it now as I did then. Literally a hush fell on the room, and every eye at the table, be it young or old, would follow that man from the door to the desk. No other figure of the theatre of that epoch or perhaps of any other would command that.'

Perhaps the most significant words in that extract are 'quite unselfconsciously', for though Bancroft lays no special emphasis on them, he is here corroborating the explanation of Irving's way given by Craig, which is that Irving made the impression he did simply because he was so much of a piece that he gave no thought at all to what that impression might be. He was, Craig suggests, at all times and in all places simply an actor, 'who never allowed any other thought than the stage to enter his head':

If he sat in a garden, the garden became a stage. Any point in the garden that might be of any slight value to him later on he made a mental note of. When making this mental note he had a peculiarly concentrated, yet far-away look about him. . . It was not put on—not acting in that sense—but it was such a concentrated essence of love for that to which he had devoted his soul that it became positively terrifying, unless by chance you knew what it was he was thinking of, seeing, hearing, and noting.

It was this strange way of his which people felt to be mysterious, for people seldom encountered such singleness of purpose. It is not easy to conceive a person who from morn until night shall think of one thing only, see one thing only, and allude to everything in terms of that one thing. . . .

It meant the whole of this world and the next, with Irving, to be an ACTOR, and in his innocence, his proud innocence, he supposed it meant as much to every other performer. I would go so far as to say that so intense was the fire which burned in him, this belief of his that the ACTOR was all that really mattered, that he suffered keenly whenever he found actors taking things easily, and considering too lightly this thing which to him was really a sacred trust. It seems queer to you—maybe it even sounds a little foolish; but believe me, you who never knew him, it was just this concentrated fanatical joy, bound tight under the control of his immense will, which made him the great being he was—the superlatively great actor many of us knew him to be.

Craig stood a little closer to Irving than most people who have written about him, and is here looking a little deeper than they could. Though he admits he is guessing, his guess is based on knowledge, and rings true. Irving in ordinary life was always an actor, but not in the least in the sense in which Garrick was said by Goldsmith to be. The difference was that Garrick, for all his devotion to his art, was not singly devoted to it; he had other ambitions—to be a social success, and a rich man. So had Kean, and so had Mrs Siddons, and so had such other aspirants to greatness as Kemble and Macready. For sheer selfless devotion to his art, then, Irving stands out alone even in the highest rank of the acting profession.

It was a fortunate thing for our theatre that such a man came exactly when he did. The mid-Victorian generation liked its great men to look and behave like important personages, and from the highest statesmen down to the humblest father of a family the men of the period did their best, each in his own sphere, to act the part assigned to them. Often they failed, and even when they succeeded their performances do not always look very convincing to their successors. But Irving, the professional actor, was one of those who did not have to act; he seemed an important personage because he was one, and therefore he was able to have the theatre acknowledged, both among the arts and in social relations, in a way which would have been impossible to anybody less impressive. That he was the first actor to look forward to a time when the theatre might be given official recognition in the form of a subsidized National Theatre is merely an accident of history; for to all his predecessors since the Restoration, doomed as they were to exist on sufferance both in private and in public, such a thing would have seemed mere wishful thinking. But Irving did more than turn men's minds to the idea of a National Theatre—he gave them ocular proof how valuable such an institution might be. For there was a sense in which the Lyceum under Irving's management took the place of a National Theatre just as, much later and under very different auspices, the Old Vic took that place. And this came about neither through pressure of historical events nor because any hitherto unexpressed public desire for such an institution was now finding expression, but simply because the prestige and character of Henry Irving had made of himself and his theatre a source of national pride.

SIR HENRY IRVING (1838–1905)
from the portrait by Sir John Millais

An artist's impression of the audience at a performance by Sir Henry Irving in 1880

Chapter 11

IRVING'S WAY

HENRY IRVING DIED IN 1905, AND THEREFORE THE PLAYGOERS who saw him when they were young are not yet very old, as old age is reckoned to-day. I could have seen him myself, for I was fifteen and a devoted playgoer at the time of his death; but though fortune did not put this in my way, I was, without exactly knowing it, very conscious of his existence. Those were days in which parties of friends, lacking mechanical means of amusing themselves, used to spend a good deal of their time amusing each other, The amateur wag was in great demand—it is on record that my mother once issued to an assistant master at my first school the terrifying invitation to come to tea and be funny—and every amateur wag had an imitation of Henry Irving in his repertoire. Is was an understood thing, too, that if a beach entertainer struck a highly unnatural attitude and spoke in a sepulchral voice he, and consequently his audience, had Irving somewhere in mind, As late as 1932, on a pleasure cruise, I heard a very stagey-looking passenger (who was in fact the proprietor of a small cinema-theatre) dubbed 'Henry Irving' by somebody as he came aboard, and the name had been adopted by everybody else within a matter of hours, These are straws, but they show clearly enough which way the wind has been blowing, and still blows. Irving stands, for those who never saw him, as the very type of the artificial actor. Consequently, he has come to be regarded by a younger generation of playgoers, trained to worship realism in acting, not only as an artificial actor but as a very bad one by their standards.

'If Irving came back to the stage now, should we think him a great actor?'—the question has often been put during the post-Irving age, that period of interesting plays and level acting which will probably go down to theatrical history as the Shaw Era; and nobody who asked the question realized that it was a test not of Irving but of the public. On this point, Craig is quite explicit:

'But was he natural?' is always being asked. Indeed he was—natural like lightning—but not natural like the ape. Some there are who will for ever think that to be commonplace is to be natural. They find it very natural in an actor to drift on and off the stage, or tactfully to avoid saying or doing anything that might astonish anyone in the audience. . . . To these, then, it must appear that if an actor is expressive he is unnatural; if he astonishes, he is positively eccentric; if he is dramatic, a scandal.

Irving was astonishing us always—he was terrible in tragedy; not terrifying as a sudden thunderclap, but as when the whole of nature seems to suffer and to become more still and more and more quiet, so did Irving do. There is a flash—something is struck—something terrible has happened, without rumblings or crash. These come afterwards; then the clouds conspire and, like a crowd of actors, create a fearful noise—but the tragedy, the terrible thing, has happened. The force which struck and blinded us has withdrawn, and is once again veiled within its secret temple. Irving in tragedy was not like the storm which splutters out, but like the one which gathers and then strikes—once. Once aware of this we were awake.

Again, Irving was natural, yet highly artificial. He was natural in that he did not remind one of an ape or a god, but of a man. He was artificial as certain plants seem artificial—we don't call them artificial flowers, for they are alive and growing. And Irving was artificial as these—as an orchid, as a cactus—exotic and stately, forbidding, and so curiously composed as to be what we call architectural—attractive as are all shapely things. Every moment was formed.

It will be seen at once how directly this description challenges the views of Irving's acting held by prominent critics of his day, notably William Archer and Bernard Shaw. To these two men Irving and his methods, and still more the popular success which those methods enjoyed, constituted a menace to the theatre, a stumbling-block to its progress. They were the apostles of a new, realistic theatre, in which the dramatist, not the actor, should be king; a theatre of ideas rather than emotions, first made to seem possible by the emergence of Ibsen, the obscure and shocking Norwegian dramatist whose works Archer translated and whose virtues Shaw trumpeted abroad. Irving, with his tremendous force and his mannerisms, did not fit into any Archer-Shaw scheme of things as they ought to be. He was reaction personified, a deplorable symbol of bad old days. With complete honesty they set themselves to cure the public of its strange prepossession in Irving's favour. Archer gravely deplored him—his way of speaking, which could not be called the King's English, his means of progression, which was certainly not to be described as walking. Shaw mocked him, and the brilliance of that mockery still dazzles the eyes of the generation of critics and playgoers to which I belong, making it difficult for any of us to see past its distorting mirror to the real Irving.

For Craig the distorting mirror does not exist. 'Mr Shaw has always been a sincere enemy to the Theatre, and one who inno-

cently bears false witness against most artists', he says, and pushes
Shaw aside—a superb gesture for a man writing in 1930, with the
Shaw Era at its peak. How far he is justified in his remark about
Shaw's hostility is matter for examination in a later chapter. Here
we are concerned with his refutation of the Archer-Shaw charge
that Irving could neither walk nor speak properly; and the first
witness against Irving is Irving himself. Ellen Terry in her memoirs
has this passage:

Once when I was touring with him in America, at the time when he was at the
highest point of his fame, I watched him one day in the train—always a delightful occupation, for his face provided many pictures a minute—and being struck
by a curious look, half puzzled, half despairing, asked him what he was thinking about. 'I was thinking', he answered slowly, 'how strange it is that I should
have made the reputation I have as an actor, with nothing to help me—with no
equipment. My legs, my voice, everything has been against me. For an actor
who can't walk, can't talk, and has no face to speak of, I've done pretty well.'

Craig, though he quotes that passage, will have none of it as
evidence. In effect, he asks the court for leave to treat Irving as a
hostile witness, and uses his own eloquence to prove him so.
Granted that Irving's gait on the stage was unusual, every movement was calculated and effective, and in private life his walk was
like anybody else's. Granted that he pronounced words in a way
of his own, particularly when he was excited; the effect was to
make them more striking, and to emphasize their meaning. And
if he had no face to speak of, that was because he had converted it into
that much more expressive thing, an actor's mask, which shows
only what he means it to show. As proof of all that he says, Craig gives
a lengthy and characteristically discursive description of Irving's
method in the opening scene of *The Bells*, which is so much to my
purpose that I give it here almost in full:

At his entrance the applause was so instantaneous that it became part of the
play. . . In *The Bells*, the hurricane of applause at Irving's entrance was no in-
terruption. It was no boisterous greeting by an excitable race for a blustering
actor—it was something which can only be described as part and parcel of the
whole, as right as rain. It was a torrent while it lasted. Power responded to
power. This applause was no false note, whereas silence would have been
utterly false; for though Irving endured and did not accept the applause, he
deliberately called it out of the spectators. It was necessary *to them*—not to him;
it was something they had to experience, or be rid of, or rather released from,
before they could exactly take in what he was going to give them.
    So then the applause came down like thunder as Irving appeared in the door-
way with the ordinary cry: 'It is I.' Now no one has ever been known to hear
these words distinctly—they resolved themselves into a single exclamation.

The door is flung open, the figure is in the room, God knows how—with arms extended, face alight, and this single exclamation: ' It is I.' . . . I can only speak of Irving's entrances, but I believe that with Edmund Kean an entrance was also something to experience. The *manner of coming on* made it extraordinary with great actors—it was this manner of timing the appearance, measuring its speed and direction, which created a rhythm that was irresistible. An exit was important too—very important: but the going off of an actor was nothing comparable to the prime importance of his coming on.

To prepare for this entrance in *The Bells* the entire first fifteen minutes of the play conspired. . . . Irving once on, the shout of applause going up, he lowers his arms, he lowers his head, he relaxes his force all over, seems to turn it off to an almost dead calm, while the applause rolls on and up. Twice, maybe three times, he, as it were, shifts one foot (his right I think it was), and by this slight and meaningless gesture a limit is being reckoned to the applause which goes on and on—no other motion, except that the foot in shifting sends a slight vibration, also without significance, through the whole person before us—and then as the applause dies away, at the first sign of it dying, the actor clips it off by a sudden gesture of awakening from his long and patiently endured ordeal —flings cap and whip to right and left, and begins to shed his coat, his muffler, as his wife and daughter run to help him off with them.

Here Craig digresses to tell his readers the plot of the play—how Mathias, now a solid citizen, once murdered a Polish Jew for his money, and is always hearing the bells of the Jew's sleigh ringing in his mind. The description of Irving in the part then goes on:

The thing Irving set out to do was to show us the sorrow which slowly and remorselessly beat him down. As, no matter who the human being may be, and what his crime, the sorrows which he suffers must appeal to our hearts, so Irving set out to wring our hearts, not to give us a clever exhibition of antics such as a murderer would be likely to go through. He does not appeal to any silly sentimentality in you—he merely states the case by showing you that quite obviously here is a strong human being who, through a moment of weakness, falls into error and becomes for two hours a criminal—does what he knows he is doing—acts deliberately—but (and here is Irving) acts automatically, as though compelled by an immense force, against which no resistance is possible.

To return to the moment after the first entrance . . . you might think that the act of taking off some boots could be done in one way only—but the way Irving did it had never been thought of till he did it, and has never been done since. It was, in every gesture, every half move, in the play of his shoulders, legs, head, and arms, mesmeric in the highest degree—slowly we were drawn to watch every inch of his work as we are drawn to read and linger on every syllable of a strangely fine writer. It was the perfection of craftsmanship.

While he is taking off the boots and pulling on the shoes the men at the table, who are smoking and drinking lazily, are telling in drawling tones that just before he came in they were saying that they did not remember a winter like this since what was called the Polish Jew's winter.

By the time the speaker had got this slowly out—and it was dragged purposely—Irving was buckling his second shoe, seated, and leaning over it with

his two long hands stretched down over the buckles. We suddenly saw these
fingers stop their work; the crown of the head suddenly seemed to glitter and
become frozen—and then, at the pace of the slowest and most terrified snail,
the two hands, still motionless and dead, were seen to be coming up the side of
the leg . . . the whole torso of the man, also seeming frozen, was gradually,
and by an almost imperceptible movement, seen to be drawing up and back,
as it would straighten a little, and to lean a little against the back of the chair
on which he was seated.

Once in that position—motionless—eyes fixed ahead of him and fixed on us
all—there he sat for the space of ten or twelve seconds, which, I can assure you,
seemed to us all like a lifetime, and then said—and said in a voice deep and
overwhelmingly beautiful: 'Oh, you were talking of that, were you?' And as the
last word was uttered, there came afar off the regular throbbing of sledge-bells.

There he sat looking at us, and there sat the others, smoking and musing
and comfortably motionless, except for the smoke from their pipes—and on
and on went the sound of these bells, on and on and on—nothing else. Again, I
assure you, that time seemed out of joint and moved as it moves to us who suffer
when we wish it would move on and it does not stir.

And the next step of his dance began.

This metaphor of the dance runs through all Craig's elucida-
tions of Irving's art. It is a counterblast to Archer's complaint that
the actor's stage gait could not be called walking. Of course it could
not, says Craig; it was not walking, it was a set and formalized
pattern of movement, like a dance—and after a little he uses
'dance' no longer as a figure of speech, but as if he meant it for an
exact picture of Irving's movement. Now he goes on to tell how
Irving looked about him to find out if anybody but himself were
listening to the bells. Then:

A long pause, endless, breaking our hearts, comes down over everything, and
on and on go these bells. Puzzled, motionless . . . he glides up to a standing
position: never has anyone seen another rising figure which slid slowly up like
that. With one arm slightly raised, with sensitive hand speaking of far-off appre-
hended sounds, he asks, in the voice of some woman who is frightened yet does
not wish to frighten those with her: 'Don't you . . . don't you hear the sound of
sledge-bells on the road?'

But the others have not heard it, and say so drowsily:

Suddenly he staggers, and shivers from his toes to his neck; his jaws begin to
chatter; the hair on his forehead, falling over a little, writhes as though it were
a nest of little snakes. Every one is on his feet at once to help: 'Caught a chill . . .
let's get him to bed' . . . and one of the movements of the immense and touch-
ing dance closes—only one—and the next one begins and the next after—figure
after figure of exquisite pattern and purpose is unfolded, and then closed, and
ever a new one unfolded in its wake.

I can write no more; you may perhaps have felt something. I don't know—

but, if you did, I know that it was one-thousandth part of what we felt. As we watched this figure we felt as silent and as still as when we hear of things too sad to realize; and when it was over and we might move, we knew that this was the finest point that the craft of acting could reach.

It is perhaps worth emphasizing that throughout this description Craig is speaking simply as a member of the audience, not as a member of Irving's company. He himself never played in *The Bells*, and never watched a rehearsal at the Lyceum of any play in which he was not taking part. To do so, he says, is in the nature of an intrusion. But between 1889 and 1900 he saw Irving act in it, he thinks, more than thirty times, and his tribute, being that of an exceptionally privileged and exceptionally gifted playgoer, may be accepted as a true description of Irving's effect on the more responsive members of his audiences. But it is easy to understand why Archer and Shaw could not be among those more responsive members. They were heading a movement towards serious playwriting that was to be more intellectual and less emotional than serious playwriting had ever been before, and it was clear that to an actor of Irving's emotional power such a movement could have no interest at all. An Irving simply did not care whether the plays in which he appeared were well-written or carefully thought out, so long as they gave him actable characters in telling situations. It is notable that in that scene described above by Craig the writer of the play comes in for none of the credit, and indeed had not written one word of dialogue that could not have been put out by the merest hack. To such an actor as Irving, an adequately well-written melodrama such as *The Bells*, or a crudely written melodrama such as *The Lyons Mail*, or even a blank-verse play like *Louis XI* vamped from the French by Dion Boucicault, who was a pitiful poet, was material almost as effective as the best of Shakespeare.

For the moment, Irving had the victory. Archer was read with respect and Shaw with shocked amusement, but the public flocked to see Irving, and paid him the finest compliment that an actor can receive—they rose at him. Only the other day a playgoing friend of mine told me wistfully how his father had been a member of an Irving audience which, at a certain point in the play, found itself so pulled by the actor's sheer power that it rose as one man to its feet without knowing till afterwards that it had done so. Kean achieved this the first time he played Overreach, and the story is that when he got home to his wife she asked him, charac-

teristically, what Lord Essex—a director of Drury Lane—had
thought of him. Kean's reply, equally characteristic, was: 'Lord
Essex be damned—the pit rose at me.' Since Irving no actor has
brought an English audience to its feet, nor has any actor, according to Craig, performed the kindred exploit of bringing the house
down.

Even in the epoch of Irving it was seldom that anybody else 'brought down
the house', but Irving brought it down. A terrific sweep of applause is not
'bringing the house down'. 'Bringing the house down' is when everybody
simultaneously calls out, and applauds simultaneously and electrically. A
vast number of people can ponderously express approval, but that is not what
I mean.

You have been to the Russian Ballet perhaps on one of its great nights, or
you have heard Chaliapine's reception at Covent Garden. Well, that is not what
I mean either. Those are ovations, but mild ovations. The thing I mean had
three times the capacity of that.

Irving's victory, however, was only momentary. Long before his
career came to an end it was obvious that popular taste, for the
first time in the history of the theatre, was beginning to prefer the
art of the dramatist to that of the actor. An epigrammatic way of
putting the case would be to say that the new public preferred
Ibsen to Irving, but this would be more alliterative than accurate.
Ibsen was still unpopular, and his devotees were still regarded as
wrong-headed and probably immoral. But a new race of dramatists arrived who, without conscious recognition of their debt to
the bleak Norwegian, were clearly under his influence. Pinero at
their head—who once, as an actor, had been a member of Irving's
company—these dramatists concerned themselves in their plays
less with spectacular theatrical situations and more with the social
or domestic issues of ordinary life. Increasingly, the theatre became a place in which the 'great' actor was unprovided for;
increasingly, the audiences learned to understand and seek for
plays in which the star was no longer a solo performer but the
leader of an orchestra. As playgoers ceased to experience strong
emotion in the theatre, they lost the capacity to respond to it; and
within a very short time after Irving's death actors of Irving's
kind, but with less than Irving's power, trying to excite London
audiences to their old emotional response, were received with
nothing warmer than an embarrassed politeness. Martin Harvey,
the best of these actors, was constrained to go more and more to the
conservative provinces for recognition, and ended in a comparative
obscurity for which a knighthood can have been poor consolation.

Since, then, Irving was the last of a line of great actors whose avowed aim was not so much to convey a dramatist's idea as to wring an audience's hearts; and since that throne has been vacant and unhonoured for so long now that anybody who may ascend it in time to come will not do so as heir to it but as founder of a new dynasty; here is the place to discuss the attitude of these great virtuosi to their public, and the effect upon them of the impassioned applause which their performances evoked, and to establish, if possible, some firm conclusion. If, as I believe, great acting depends for its very existence upon the presence of a properly responsive audience, how far have its practitioners shown themselves conscious of this? How, for example, can we square Gordon Craig's description of the applause in *The Bells* as an integral and necessary part of Irving's effect, with the actor's reception of it as an ordeal, or with his statement that the artist comes to regard his audiences with 'good-natured contempt'?

We know no more of Burbage in this respect than in any other, but we have heard from Cibber that Betterton regarded a completely silent audience as a greater tribute to his powers than one which applauded him noisily. Garrick was 'of applause a mere glutton', and we have seen Mrs Siddons unable to proceed happily without the encouragement of physical response from her hearers. Kean was in the seventh heaven when the pit rose at him. Irving was of Betterton's opinion, so that we have three of our great ones avid of loud applause, and two who regard it with indifference. Is there, then, between Betterton and Irving on the one hand, and Garrick, Sarah Siddons, and Kean on the other, some fundamental difference of attitude which needs to be defined and accounted for? I think not. There is a difference, but it is superficial and depends simply on the amount of personal vanity in each individual player's make-up. Garrick was notoriously vain, and so was Kean; Mrs Siddons comes into a slightly different category because, as a beautiful woman, she had been accustomed to be praised to (and on account of) her face, and had come to expect it. Betterton and Irving were free of this vanity, Betterton perhaps because he was more sure of himself than Garrick or Kean, Irving because of that sinking of the man in the artist to which Gordon Craig has already borne witness in the last chapter.

The point therefore is not whether any one of these great players happened to like an ovation or to be merely tolerant of it, but that all five and Burbage too were equally in need of that emotional response from their audiences of which applause is merely the outward sign. Without this emotional response the artist knows that his efforts are—for that particular audience and for that particular performance—sterile and vain; but once emotional contact is made (and the actor knows instantly when it has been made) the artist is fulfilled and satisfied, and only the childish, greedy side of him yearns for the symbols of a success already obtained.

This is why so many noisy demonstrations of apparent delight by so many artificially enthusiastic first-night audiences do not create an illusion of success for a play which has failed to grip. Every sensitive and experienced playgoer, and in particular every established drama critic, knows without waiting for applause to tell him whether the actors and the audience have made emotional contact or not, exactly in the same degree, and for very much the same reason, as a fish knows whether or not it has been hooked. If he knows that the audience of which he is part has refused the proffered bait, he merely resents attempts on the part of the management and its friends to persuade him otherwise.

It is to the *Diaries* of Macready that we must look for the clearest evidence of the effect of an audience upon an actor. Although I have taken Macready's claim to greatness, for the purpose of this book, as not proven, he was the leading tragedian of his time and his right to speak may be accepted without hesitation. Also, his remarks on the subject of audiences are passing comments, made not to establish a theory but to record an impression. What is more, they are scattered freely over the whole period of nearly twenty years (1833–51) which the *Diaries* cover. They are therefore an extremely valuable body of evidence, all the more valuable because they were written by an exceedingly hot-tempered man on a subject on which he had no inducement either to hide his feelings or to mince his words. Macready was an actor by inheritance, training, and temperament, but unlike Irving (whose rise to fame he lived to see, for he did not die till 1873) he did not bless the fate that had made him so. He had been educated at Rugby and intended for one of the gentlemanly professions when his father's financial collapse and sudden death had ruined his hopes, and in consequence he deeply resented the social snubs to which, as an actor, he was forced to submit. Equally deeply he disliked the tawdriness inseparable from the theatre, and was delighted when he could escape from it to his adored family in the comfortable country house, at which the neighbours were doubtful whether they should call. Perhaps this division of mind prevented him from being an unquestionably great player; but at least it makes him a witness not likely to exaggerate the importance to his art of a responsive audience. If ever there was an actor formed by temperament to treat his public with a lofty disdain it was Macready. Yet he could not. Again and again the plain fact emerges that upon the quality of the audience depends the effectiveness of the actor.

Macready's special *bête noire* was that same unimpressionable Edinburgh audience against whose armour Mrs Siddons had blunted her best shafts. It was as impervious in his day as it had been in hers, and it drove him to fury again and again. According to its maddening custom, it concealed a considerable admiration under an appearance of critical detachment, and once at the end of a season, when it paid him the compliment of calling for him, Macready did not appear because he had put on his cloak and left the theatre the instant he was free to do so. He notes the fact in his diary with some satisfaction, and inquires rhetorically what he could possibly have to say to an Edinburgh audience. But in 1850, when he was near his early retirement while still at the height of his powers, he began, a little late, to understand Scots reserve. The italics are Macready's, not mine:

Edinburgh, March 18th. Acted *Macbeth*—*one* of the best, as among the *most complete* representations I have ever given of the character. The audience, who were disposed to be friendly, but do not seem *used to applaud much*, became warmed into something like deep interest and enthusiasm as the play proceeded. I left no weak points in it. Called, and very warmly applauded.

To a London audience he could on occasion be grateful and generous, as is shown by the following sentences from the entry for 7 December 1841:

Went to the Haymarket Theatre. Acted Claude Melnotte with vigour, gaiety, and energy, inspired and animated by the good house and the feeling they displayed towards me—perhaps I never acted it better; it was the *last time*. Was called for and very enthusiastically received. I bowed my adieux.

This, from an American tour, shows the actor in a belligerent mood, but none the less defeated:

Charleston, January 8th, 1844. Acted Hamlet, I scarcely know how. I strove and fought up against what I thought the immobility of the audience; I would not be beaten cravenly, but such a performance is never satisfactory—at least to the actor. When he is contending with the humour of his audience, adieu then to all happy moments, to all forgetfulness of self, to the *élan* of enthusiasm. I died game, for I tried to sustain myself to the last. Called for.

In the autumn of the year following, however, at Leicester, he had the most galling experience of all, which drove him to thoughts of the early grave he was constantly expecting but never attained; he lived to be eighty.

September 30th, 1845. Acted Hamlet well—I think *very well* to a *very wretched* house. These things will prey upon me; I am not proof to them; they prolong my term of servitude—of bondage, and life has very few pleasures or enjoyments for me. I do not know, but I think I should not care much to quit it. *God guide me!*

But it was in 1851, just before his retirement, that he became most outspoken. Here are two entries for consecutive days, which show how his estimate of his audience varied:

January 22nd. Acted Iago with a vigour and discrimination that I have never surpassed, if ever equalled. . . . That last performance of Iago was, in my mind, a commentary on the text, an elucidation and an opening out of the profound conception of that great creative mind, Shakespeare, which has not been given before in the inward feeling of the part: the selfishness, sensuality and delight in the exercise of his own intellectual power I have never seen in Cooke or Young, nor read of in Henderson, as being so developed. I don't believe . . . that they penetrated beyond the surface of the part. . . . But what is the difference to an audience? To how many among them does the deep reflection, the toil of thought, carried out into the most animated and energetic personation, speak its own necessary course of labour? By how many among them is the 'poor' player, who devotes himself to his art, appreciated—where are the intelligences capable of understanding his author or himself? Is Prince Albert one? Is Queen Victoria one? . . .

Jan. 23rd. Acted Benedict [*sic*]—as well as I could with a most unfit representative of Beatrice, and two stupid dolts in the Prince and Claudio, that almost baffled every attempt I made to be understood. It was only when I was *alone* in the garden scene that I could *assert myself* before my audience, and that they could *satisfactorily respond* to me.

So the pendulum swung back and forth. But as we read, the impression grows that perhaps Macready was right to despise the audiences of his day. 'I have in Hamlet', he says, 'worked against prejudice and against stubborn ignorance, and it has been a labour of love with me.' Dismiss that if you like as a vain man's attempt to justify himself by blaming others for his failure; but do not deny that there may be truth in it.

For myself, I believe that there is a great deal of truth in it. We have seen how much of their greatness all the great players owed to their luck in being born at a time when the public was ready and able to accept what each of them had to give. If Macready had had similar luck, instead of living at a time when our theatre had little life and no freshness of ideas, he might have cut a different figure. Because he complained too much, because he denounced as an unprincipled scoundrel almost anybody with whom he did not see precisely eye to eye, because he used the sanctimonious mid-Victorian vocabulary to express his private thoughts, Macready in his *Diaries* often seems a self-satisfied prig. I believe he was more, much more, than that; an actor who might have become truly great if his audiences had let him.

Chapter 12

The Actor's Magic

AND SO THE PAGEANT HAS GONE BY, AND AS ITS LAST IMPRESSIVE figure dwindles in the distance there may perhaps remain for you who have seen it pass—as most certainly for me who set it in motion —a heightened sense of continuity. We have seen six players who, each in his own time and before his appropriate audience, have come nearest to complete realization of the tragic actor's highest ambition—to wring men's hearts. In themselves they were people of widely different character and method; but seen at close quarters with one another they have likenesses more striking, and for my present purposes infinitely more important, than their differences. Any speculations based on their dissimilarities must be fruitless, but if we consider the characteristics which the great players had in common we may possibly arrive at some conclusion not purely academic; though whether by such methods we can hope to put together a composite portrait of the Great Actor is more than doubtful.

Certainly the Great Actor need not be very much to look at, at any rate to the casual eye. Even if we discard the tradition that Burbage was fat, he remains short. Betterton was 'not exceeding the middle stature, inclining to the corpulent'. Garrick, to Partridge's innocent gaze, was just a little frightened man. Kean was too small, everybody thought, to be taken seriously as a tragedian. Irving's physical disadvantages were a matter of common remark. Nor is it seriously claimed on behalf of any one of these five men that he had a handsome face; their eulogists avoid that question pointedly, and take refuge in the implication that beauty is, after all, only skin deep. Mrs Siddons had an impressive figure and was acclaimed a beauty; but her good looks were not one of her major assets, for Gainsborough grumbled while painting her that there was no end to her nose, and she herself said that the long Kemble jaw was a dreadful handicap to a woman. The Great Actor, then, may be of almost any shape of body or cast of countenance; but all the evidence goes to show that he will have one remarkable feature—

his eyes. Burbage must be taken for granted in this respect, as in so many others; and Betterton's 'serious and penetrating aspect' is only given passing reference by Cibber, who was obsessed with the idea that nothing much mattered in an actor but his voice. But I have already produced evidence, which I need not recapitulate here, to show that each one of the other four had the power of conveying the most intense emotions through the eyes alone. Nor need the Great Actor have a specially captivating voice. There have been many actors of high rank whose voices had music in them—Forbes-Robertson, Martin Harvey, and Henry Ainley come at once to my mind, among those whom I have listened to —but among the really great players it seems to be the effect rather than the sound of the voice that is striking. There is always a danger, as Ainley showed, that the actor who knows that his voice is a fine organ will use it as a musical instrument and forget the sense of the words he is speaking, and so perhaps it is significant that none of the greatest players has had to face this temptation. Betterton's voice was 'more manly than sweet', Garrick's seldom called for special mention and is not specifically referred to as one of his professional assets in Lichtenberg's long catalogue, Sarah Siddons's struck Parson Bate unfavourably when he first heard it, Kean's was never very good and was more and more affected by brandy as time went on, Irving's was constantly getting him into trouble with critics. All we can postulate of the Great Actor's voice, then, is enough flexibility to make it able to express his emotions as well as his meaning, and enough volume to make it as audible as he wishes.

The only other physical attribute that these great players have in common is strength—not the spiritual force which may exist in a puny body, but plain ordinary muscular power and control. I once asked a friend of mine who is a notable all-round athlete why games came so easily to him, and he answered promptly that it was simply because he was only five feet eight inches in height, which meant that his centre of gravity was low, and he was therefore free from that tendency to top-heaviness against which bigger men had to struggle; in other words, his balance was naturally perfect. What he could do with grace and ease, other less fortunate men had with difficulty to learn to do. The point was made in casual conversation, and at the time it did not occur to me that what was true of the games-player was even more true of the actor. Balance and muscular control are relatively of more importance on the stage even than on the cricket-field, the golf-course, or the tennis-court. Many an awkward-looking player of games has contrived to compensate for his lack of grace, and to win the highest honours over the heads of his more stylish competitors; but an actor can only be what he appears to be, since his whole concern is with *seeming*. This being so, it is perhaps not altogether a coincidence that the only man among our great players who was above middle height was Henry Irving, and that he alone among them felt himself not to be in full enough control of his powers to face a London audience until after—and well after—his thirtieth birthday. Even then, as we have seen, his style was unorthodox and to many, awkward and ugly; a Gordon Craig was needed to point out that however it may have looked, his body was under perfect control.

Apart from Irving, all the men were of the natural games-player's build—short, sturdy, and balanced. This, in fact, is almost all we know for certain of Burbage's appearance. Betterton had 'limbs nearer the athletic than the delicate proportion'. Kean, only five feet three inches tall, was a trained acrobat who retained his ability to tumble long after he had established himself as the leading tragedian of the day. As for Garrick, this is how he struck Lichtenberg in the year 1775—and as you read the passage, remember that Lichtenberg is describing a Garrick nearly sixty years of age, who within a year will retire from the stage and in a little more than three years will die of a complication of painful diseases:

His stature is rather low than of middle height, and his body thickset. His limbs are in the most pleasing proportion, and the whole man is put together most charmingly. Even the eye of the connoisseur cannot remark any defect either in his limbs, in the manner they are knit, or in his movements. In the latter one is enchanted to observe the fullness of his strength, which, when shown to advantage, is more pleasing than extravagant gestures.

. . . It gives one a sense of freedom and well-being to observe the strength and certainty of his movements and what complete control he has over the muscles of his body. . . . In the scene in *The Alchemist* where he boxes, he runs about and skips from one neat leg to the other with such admirable lightness that one would dare swear that he was floating in the air.

In a later letter the same observer adds a shrewd footnote to this description:

The indescribably pleasing lightness, vigour and certainty of movement . . . in which Mr Garrick excels were not, I expect, acquired without difficulty, although I will not deny that the excellent proportion of his limbs helped to produce them. I fear that many years and much grilling labour went towards the

exercising of his body, before it attained at length to this effortless ease, which
. . . now looks as if it came to him naturally.

We have only to compare this description with eye-witness accounts
of other actors to see that Garrick's grace was something peculiarly
his own, not necessarily to be expected of other players on his own
exalted level. The visual beauty of Garrick's movements was a
happy accident of nature; the important point about them—and
I do not feel that Lichtenberg would have disagreed with this if the
question had been raised—was not their accidental and inherent
beauty, but their controlled strength which, as the German professor did not fail to record, was far from accidental.

This point has special importance with reference to Irving,
because his contemporary detractors lost sight of it altogether.
When William Archer, as an unknown writer twenty-one years of
age, sounded his first challenge to the general view that Irving's
work at the Lyceum had put him among the great, he did it by
collaborating with Robert W. Lowe in an anonymous sixpenny
pamphlet called *The Fashionable Tragedian*; and with a youthful
cocksureness difficult to credit in the grave judicial man I knew
forty-three years later, he laid down a few simple rules for the
Great Actor—rules whose simplicity is equalled only by their
complete unsoundness:

Let us now come to the gist of our argument. The first requisite for histrionic
greatness is power to move and speak like a normal and rational human being.
A man may have intellect, 'picturesqueness', taste, and all the rest of it, but
if he walks like an automaton whose wheels need oiling, and speaks alternately
from the pit of his stomach and the top of his head, he will never be a great, or
a good, or even a passable actor.

There is here, you observe, no faintest glimmer of a notion that
an actor who can move discriminating audiences to ecstasy night
after night may be a great, must be a good, and is far more than a
passable actor, whatever his eccentricities of gait or speech. The
pamphlet goes on:

Can it be denied that Mr Irving does all this? In walking, he plants one foot
upon the stage as if his whole 'eminence' depended upon its firmness, and then
drags the other leg after it in a limp and nerveless fashion, which cannot be
described, and must be seen to be appreciated—all the while working spas-
modically with his shoulders, and very often nodding his head backwards and
forwards in a manner which is positively painful to contemplate. In speaking,
again, his naturally harsh voice is rendered still more unpleasant by his trick of
alternating between *basso profundo* and *falsetto*, like a ventriloquist imitating a

conversation between a Giant Comoran and Jack the Giant-killer. Moreover, his pronunciation of English is a study in itself.

Gordon Craig's answer to this, as I have indicated already, was that the eccentricities did not matter, since Irving had them under control and used them deliberately to get the effects he wanted. It was, and is, a complete answer, but I am doubtful whether at any time in his career Archer was capable of being convinced by it. Archer was a great critic, within the rigid limits imposed upon him by the fact that he always trusted his head and distrusted his heart. He had an utterly logical mind, and the trouble with that kind of mind is that once it has started from a wrong premiss it cannot ever be right except by abandoning the premiss. Archer and Lowe started the argument from an obviously wrong premiss in the passage above, and although Archer recognized later that there was more to be said in Irving's favour than he had thought at first, he continued to the end of his life—as the next chapter will show—to be guided too much by his intellect and too little by his emotions. He was not the first Scotsman to be afraid of his feelings.

So much for the composite portrait. I cannot pretend that it has shown us much for, except for the remarkable and expressive eyes, it might stand for a great footballer just as well as for a great actor. But at least it may serve to dispel any lingering notion that the great actor need have anything at all in common with the film star.

Now we come to the consideration of the great actor's mental and spiritual qualities, and here, since we are to move among mysteries, a different and much more wary method of approach to the subject becomes necessary. As I may at any moment find myself involved in an effort to explain the inexplicable, let me at least give myself a firm jumping-off place by stating the obvious. Here it is, then. The first mental quality that the actor needs is the power of make-believe, or, if you prefer a more dignified term, a creative imagination. Could anything be more obvious than that? And yet, when we ask ourselves what this power of make-believe is, and how it persuades the spectator to accept it, there are no obvious answers. It is in the power to get itself accepted that the actor's make-believe differs from the child's. An imaginative small boy may dress up in feathers and moccasins and war-paint and convince himself that he is an Indian chief, but unless he has a touch of the actor's creative quality he will not persuade other small boys to join in the game whole-heartedly, though they may consent to pretend out of good nature or weak-mindedness. But if the actor's touch is there, acceptance is instant and inevitable.

I once had this proved to me in the simplest possible way, when I was asked by the headmistress of a girls' county school if I would accept a professional engagement to visit her school, not as drama critic of the *Daily Telegraph*, but privately, to give my opinion of a performance of *Saint Joan* by the school's drama society. I was asked to express my views at length in a talk to the cast after the performance, and I accepted because I thought the novel experience might be good for me, though I had some misgivings whether it would turn out equally good for the girls. During the scene at the Dauphin's court my eye was caught by two players standing side by side up-stage. At the first glance there was nothing to differentiate them. Both were girls of about fourteen, both were in male dress—one as a courtier, the other as a priest—and both were looking quietly on at the scene, with nothing to say or do. Yet I suddenly noticed that these two girls were having two quite different kinds of impact on me. For no reason that could be traced home, I was accepting the 'priest' as a priest, while the 'courtier' was to me merely a dressed-up schoolgirl. In my talk to the company afterwards I related what had happened, and suggested the only explanation I could think of, that the 'priest' was thinking of herself as a priest, and was therefore mentally *in* the play, while the 'courtier' was thinking of herself as a girl in funny clothes, and was therefore out of it; and that by some kind of telepathy, or perhaps my subconscious recognition of signs too slight for conscious recording, the 'priest's' imaginative effort had registered in my open and receptive mind.

Here, surely, is something solid to go on. The true actor has by nature a quality denied to others, of imagining himself to be another person with such completeness that the image in his mind impresses itself on the minds of others. *How* this is done, or does itself, must remain mysterious, but the fact that it *is* done is not to be doubted. I instanced my schoolgirl first because she conveyed an image to me without speaking or moving or exercising any conscious art whatever; but once we take conscious art into consideration there are innumerable proofs. Often and often in the theatre, when the chief player in a scene has failed to identify himself with the part he is playing, I find my attention irresistibly drawn away from him to rest with relief and satisfaction on some secondary character. The chief player may be a beautiful woman, charmingly dressed, who in her own person, off the stage, would enchant my eye and monopolize my attention; yet if she fails to act her part my eye leaves her at once, to focus itself (let us say) upon the demure and deliberately unalluring figure of her maid, absorbedly going about her duties in the background. This, or something like it, has happened to me again and again in the course of my professional life as a playgoer, and it never loses its power to surprise; for we playgoers learn with difficulty, and believe with reluctance, that beauty by itself goes for nothing in the theatre. Yet it is so much a commonplace of experience behind the scenes that shrewd stage directors, when they have to cast the part of a beautiful woman, do not look for a woman who actually is beautiful but for an actress —often a plain and sometimes a positively ugly actress—who can give the illusion of beauty on the stage.

Given, then, this power of impersonation, which every player must have who is ambitious to be worthy of any critical consideration at all, the next question is what other qualities of mind or character are necessary to carry a man or woman higher than the rank and file of the profession. Two such qualities occur to me at once. The first is concentration, or, as Gordon Craig called it in Irving's case, single-mindedness. The second is that individual magnetism which serves as a shop-window for character, and is to-day usually called 'personality'.

Single-mindedness, and the capacity for ferocious hard work which goes with it, is a quality which leads any man with talent and physical stamina to success in his chosen profession. All the same, the artist must have more of it than most men because of the solitary nature of his work, and the actor must have more of it than most artists because his solitary work must be carried on in the midst of distractions. Kean is the significant example here. Alone among the really great players, he was a man of weak character and disreputable life. In the others, ability to do with great thoroughness anything to which they had made up their minds would not be surprising—rather the reverse. It *is* surprising in Kean—the wastrel, the drunkard, the unhappy dupe of anybody who would pander to his vices or flatter his vanity. And yet he won from his unsympathetic and ill-used wife, who would have been the first to subscribe to any catalogue of his faults, the tribute that where his art was concerned he worked and slaved beyond any actor she had ever known. For Kean, the distractions normal to his profession were magnified into temptations. Yet somehow in the midst of them he contrived to be solitary, to concentrate, to force his mind back to singleness of purpose. It must have been on those long lonely walks in the country during his years as a strolling player, walks from which he would return dog-tired and surprisingly sober, that the best of his work was done.

How Kean's thoughts ran during these walks perhaps another creative actor might know, but we who are not actors must be content to guess. We can at least tell from the results in his work, and the effect of his work on his audiences, that he was doing something more than plotting out a series of novel theatrical touches. When he thought out that new and fresh interpretation of Shylock, for example, which was later to make so deep and instantaneous an impression on his first sparse audience at Drury Lane, he was doing something more than planning to break with tradition over his dress and his wig, something more than searching through the lines of the part for new stresses and pauses that might bring out their meaning more clearly, or give them unexpected new significances. He was going through that mysterious process of identifying himself with the character, an effort of the creative imagination which, in the best actors, seems to go beyond conscious thought. He was bringing into being a Shylock who was not quite a real man and yet would be expressed in terms of the actor's own bones and blood and skin and flesh, a Shylock perhaps quite different from the Jew who was alive in Shakespeare's mind when he wrote the play, and yet conforming at every point to that Shylock so far as the words he speaks are concerned.

It can hardly have failed to be noticed how often, in the various tributes to great actors which I have quoted or referred to in this book, two words occur, the words 'natural' and 'original'. It is perhaps not quite so inevitably obvious, though I believe it is equally true, that the two words are used to mean exactly the same thing. I have already pointed out in a chapter on Garrick that the 'natural' acting which he was praised for introducing had nothing at all in common with the naturalism, more exactly called 'realism', of to-day. If we praise an actor to-day for being natural, we mean only that he seems to be behaving on the stage very much as we should expect to see him behaving in his home or the street; but when any of the line of great actors which ended with Irving is praised for being natural, it means that he has not been content to imitate other men's interpretations of a dramatic character, but has been back to nature—human nature, his own nature—and has made his own interpretation in the light of his discoveries. It may be that he has discovered nothing that his predecessors did not know, but the fact that he has found them out all over again for himself makes them fresh and new for him, and enables him to make them fresh and new for his audiences in turn.

At the moments when Garrick and Kean arrived in the London theatre, it chanced that the need for this naturalness or originality was particularly insistent. The freshness with which Garrick attacked his parts, and which appealed so instantaneously to an audience grown tired of the Cibbers and the Quins, must have been the result of much unremitting study in the period when the young man was hesitating whether to brave his family's disapproval and 'commence actor'. Kean, with less intelligence than Garrick and, we may suspect, less good habits of study, was not always able to get back to nature and never managed to achieve the earlier actor's consistency; his flashes of lightning were brilliant, but in between them were passages of very ordinary, derivative acting. It is from Kean's occasional failures rather than from Garrick's steady record of artistic integrity that we can assure ourselves that the 'natural' acting which these two players, each in his own time, restored to our stage was no happy accident but an achievement deliberately worked for.

Personality is no more the special prerogative of the actor than single-mindedness. I spoke of it above as a shop-window for character, and the figure bears scrutiny. In some businesses window-dressing is all-important and has little relation to the stocks on sale; in others, the less there is in the window the more we seem to find in the shop. Public men in every walk of life need the shop-window well filled; others can please themselves.

An actor, by the nature of his art, needs skill in window-dressing, but is not relieved thereby of the need to keep a good stock in the shop. There is a tendency to-day to exaggerate the importance of this window-dressing. It is due to the rise of the realistic school of acting in which the actor appears on the stage as himself, so to speak, and interprets a part in terms of his own 'personality' instead of disguising his 'personality' to fit the part he plays. Gerald du Maurier, for example, brought to every part that he played the same lazy grace, the same casual way of lighting a cigarette, the same attractive 'personality' which did not differ from the actual man you met in the Garrick Club except that one was a thought-out stage presentation of the other. It is not of this kind of stagified 'personality' that I am now writing but of the real thing, the honest display in the window of goods which show you exactly what the shop has on sale.

This, every good actor must have, whether, like du Maurier or Charles Hawtrey or A. E. Matthews, he sticks always to the same attractive arrangement of his window or whether, like Garrick, he takes a delight in varying the arrangement from day to day. To abandon metaphor, du Maurier never disguised himself and Garrick delighted in doing so, yet both had strong personalities. Du Maurier always presented himself as the du Maurier of private life, yet was none the less always an actor. Garrick liked to obliterate himself in his parts, yet none the less was always unmistakably Garrick. Personality, in fact, is the faculty of attracting public attention; and of all faculties it is the least predictable and the least explicable.

Possibly the most astonishing thing about personality is the immediacy of its impact. Some time in the year 1920, at a feeble play called *Mr Todd's Experiment*, I saw a short scene played by a small, dark, pale girl of twenty-one, making her first appearance on the London stage. 'She did hardly more than flash into view and be gone', I wrote of her in a subsequent *Daily Telegraph* article, 'but there was in that fleeting glimpse something that set me groping and peering in the darkness to find her name in the programme.' The name, when I found it, proved to be Meggie Albanesi, and in the few years that were to pass before her untimely death it became a name indeed. Nobody doubted her supremacy among the young actresses of her generation, and many believed her to be a great actress in the making. But when she died at twenty-four—burnt out, it seemed, by the very intensity of her spirit—greatness was still no more than a remote possibility, and a possibility, as I see it now, which never could have become an accomplished fact. She had appeared in half a dozen modern plays, in none of which was there any scope for great acting; and such was the unwillingness of audiences at that time to see favourite players in big-scale classical parts that her full power might never have been tested even if she had had the physical strength to sustain it. That is perhaps beside my immediate point, but it does help to establish that Meggie Albanesi's career, so far as it went, was a proof not necessarily of great dramatic gifts, but of character illumined by great force of personality, a personality unforgettable even now by those who felt its power.

Here we are, then, at the end of my tentative list of the Great
Actor's qualities, yet still the secret of his greatness eludes us. He
must have creative imagination, concentration, and personality,
and yet if he has no more than these things he is not necessarily
great. What power is there, beyond these things and still unmen-
tioned, which all the great ones had? Looking back over the eye-
witness descriptions of each of them, I find the answer to that question clearly inscribed again and again. It is the power, possessed
by the great player and by the great player alone, to establish
between himself and a responsive audience a complete emotional
accord. I must be very careful here to emphasize the word *accord*,
because I must not be misunderstood to mean that the actor im-
poses on his audience a complete emotional surrender. It sometimes looks like that, I know; but to speak of surrender would
mean that the audience on such occasions plays a merely passive
part, which is very far from being the case. On the quality of the
audience's response depends the quality of the player's achievement, from which it follows—and I stand by the conclusion—that
an actor can be great only when he is playing to an audience that
can let him be so. A corollary from this, which again I accept, is
that an audience more sensitive than common can, on occasion,
thrust greatness on an actor by inspiring him to find heights and
depths in himself which are normally beyond his reach.

It may be said, and often was said by James Agate, that a
playgoer of my generation, who by his own admission was born too
late to see Irving, Ellen Terry, Bernhardt or Duse at their best,
can know nothing of the power of great acting except by hearsay,
and therefore cannot write about it with authority. Sadly I have
to allow that during most of my time as a playgoer great acting has
been at a discount. Yet even my generation knows what it is to
see a great player establish between himself and a responsive
audience a complete emotional accord, though our experience was
gained outside the serious theatre. We knew it in the music halls,
and the emotion we felt was not pity, nor terror, but laughter. For
there have been great clowns in our time.

Once, in my schooldays, I set out from mid-Wales to spend a
part of a Christmas holiday with friends in Manchester. It was a
miserable, slow, six-hour journey with several changes, and a dull
toothache with which I had started deepened gradually to a raging
agony. I reached Manchester almost speechless with cold and pain,
and was rushed to a dentist, who, because it was after hours and

no anæsthetist was available, pulled out the tooth at once without gas, and hurt me quite horribly. He warned me also that the place would continue to hurt for some time, and no man ever spoke more truly. A visit to the Manchester Hippodrome had been planned, and I decided on that rather than the alternative of bed, hoping that it would distract my thoughts; but turn succeeded unregarded turn, while I nursed my cheek and thought of nothing but my sufferings. Then the curtain rose and George Robey walked on to the stage. I had never seen him before, and I roused myself to a lacklustre interest . . . and twenty minutes later, when the curtain had fallen, and I had wiped my eyes and had followed my hosts to the street in a kind of daze, it occurred to me that once, long ago, as it seemed in another world, I had had toothache. Gingerly I felt the place with my tongue . . . my toothache had gone, and did not come back. If I had dared, I should have written at once to Robey to tell him what he had done; but it was many years afterwards when, meeting him at a stage party, I did tell him. I do not think I have ever seen an actor more deeply pleased at a tribute, nor with better reason.

Yet one point must be made very clear. It was not Robey himself who cured me, but Robey and his audience. If I had been alone in the theatre that night, Robey's performance might have made me laugh in spite of my pain, but I do not think that it would have charmed the pain away. That miracle was brought about because I had merged my identity in that of the audience, and had exchanged the grief of being a suffering individual for the joy of being one of a laughing crowd. Robey was, of course, the direct cause of this integration of his audience, but he was only indirectly the cause of the pull which the audience exercised on me, causing me to forget my pain and become part of itself. This 'pull' of the audience depends on the degree not of the performer's power but of the audience's integration, and in an exceptionally responsive audience it can be exercised even when nothing of special moment is happening on the stage. A friend of mine (A. R. Rawlinson, the scenario-writer and dramatist) once had an experience at the Abbey Theatre, Dublin, which proves this. He was delayed, and arrived a little late for the first act of Lennox Robinson's *The Big House*. Although the performance had only just begun, the house was tense and quiet, and the spectators were following the action with such absorbed interest that they were leaning forward in their seats. My friend sat down—and instantly, before he had even had time to take in what was going on on the stage, he found himself leaning forward like the rest, drawn by a force which he found impossible to resist.

Not many audiences, however, can have the power to integrate themselves in this way, and perhaps only the specialized following of a particular theatre—like that of the Old Vic in the 1920's— has the chance to generate that power. An ordinary audience, consisting of a number of strangers come together at haphazard, can be welded into a single entity only when it is called upon to respond to a great performer.

This, then, is the Great Actor's secret, that he can feel an emotion so intensely, express it so vividly, and share it with his audience so completely, that he turns a crowd of strangers, for the moment, into a sentient being. How this comes about is beyond explanation, either by the actor himself or by anybody else. But what cannot be explained can at least be understood. I do not find it hard to grasp that if a young schoolgirl, without experience and without conscious art, merely by thinking herself into a character can make me accept her as a medieval priest, then a Great Actor, performing the same act of imagination at a pitch of mental concentration and emotional sympathy infinitely more intense, can do with a receptive audience what he will.

Chapter 13

STAGE INTO PULPIT: THE SHAW ERA

IT IS GENERALLY ACCEPTED TO-DAY THAT IBSEN WAS THE prime cause of the revolution in dramatic writing which took place in the third quarter of the nineteenth century. He showed that plays of importance could be written about people of no importance, that the lofty theme had not necessarily to be expressed in lofty language, and that the convention of realism, hitherto sparingly used by dramatists and almost entirely confined to light comedy and satire, could be employed for plays of the utmost seriousness. As soon as his work began to be known in England, through the translations of William Archer and others, it caused an intellectual uproar. The ultra-respectable were deeply shocked at the nature of Ibsen's themes, the liberal-minded were equally deeply delighted by his moral courage and intellectual honesty. The English theatre, however, held aloof. For reasons neither moral nor intellectual, but purely social, English playgoers did not like Ibsen's plays, never have liked them, and do not like them now. I once commented on this in an apologetic tone to a Norwegian acquaintance; and all he said was: 'Why should you like them? We do not like them much in Norway, either.'

However that may be to-day, there is no doubt at all that to London playgoers of the late 'eighties and early 'nineties of the last century the Ibsen drama seemed dreary in the extreme. Most of Ibsen's characters counted in their own society as people of substance; but to the inhabitants of the capital of the immensely wealthy England of those days, they seemed provincial—or, worse, suburban—and therefore uninteresting. Nora Helmer's tarantella, and the bottle of champagne so plainly symbolizing an unusual gaiety, merely added gloom to the pervading small-town atmosphere. London audiences have never at any time taken kindly to serious foreign plays in their original settings; even at the time when our theatre was completely under the domination of Paris, and English dramatists had lost all impulse to think out plays for themselves, the imported French plays had to be given a distinctive

English dress before the public would accept them. Perhaps if Archer had adapted *A Doll's House* instead of translating it, had turned Nora into Lady Nora Helvellyn, the high-spirited daughter of a duke, and Torvald into something important in the financial world, the result would have been a long West End run. But Ibsen was too big and Archer too respectful for this; and after a production at the Criterion in 1891 nobody dared to present this play in London for twenty years.

But although Ibsen himself was caviare to the general, his indirect influence on our theatre was profound. English audiences had always had a taste for realism as a stage convention, and all through our theatrical history we find them reacting favourably to it. Shakespeare, to the delight of his public though to the horror of later formalists like Voltaire, had introduced a pair of realistic low-comedy grave-diggers into his subtlest and most exalted tragedy. Farquhar's 'pert, low dialogue' displeased his critics but delighted the pit. Goldsmith's *She Stoops to Conquer* could only with difficulty be cast by Colman at Drury Lane, so shocked were the actors by the homeliness of its style; but public acclaim put it straight into the regular repertory. Sheridan, in *The School for Scandal*, four years later, showed that natural dialogue could be used with great effect in a play not written merely to amuse. And when English playwriting broke its French fetters nearly one hundred years later, Robertson's comedies—stilted enough to us, but considered miracles of realism in their time—found the same ready welcome.

Accordingly, though Ibsen's plays could not get a proper hearing, and Ibsen's one avowed disciple, Bernard Shaw, fared no better, the popular dramatists of the time—men like Pinero and Henry Arthur Jones—found much to learn in Ibsen's methods. Both these men began their careers as dramatists by writing highly artificial plays according to the accepted conventions; both took to heart the example which the Ibsen controversy brought to their notice and began to choose more serious themes and to handle them in a more realistic way. The result was an immense improvement both in the technique of playwriting and in the taste of the audiences for new plays.

In this movement for better plays Irving took no share. The new kind of serious high comedy did not call for great solo performances by great players, but for accomplished concerted performances by accomplished players; and Irving was, or considered himself, a soloist only. Pinero, once an actor in Irving's company, never wrote a part for his old chief to play. Barrie, who wrote his first plays on Irving's advice and owed it to Irving that J. L. Toole produced them, actually wrote *The Professor's Love Story* with Irving in mind; but Irving did not see himself in the part (in which his son, H. B. Irving, later scored a great success) and gave it to E. S. Willard. Even Shaw tried to fit him out with a part, and wrote *The Man of Destiny* for him; but Irving refused it.

This lack of elasticity, or of versatility, on Irving's part was a very bad thing for the stage. Its effect on the public was to divide the late Victorian and Edwardian theatre into two; an actor's theatre, growing rapidly more and more out of date as Irving grew older, and a dramatist's theatre, growing more and more subtle and interesting as its practitioners grew more and more skilled in the use of their fascinating new medium, the realistic convention. Little by little, audiences lost touch with the old masterpieces. They were not realistic, therefore they were not worth attention— or rather, they were worth attention only so far as they could be treated realistically. Beerbohm Tree had the popular taste on his side when, in 1905 and 1911, he introduced real rabbits and a real stream into the wood in *A Midsummer Night's Dream*; but Granville Barker's 1914 production, with its fantastication and its direct appeal for imaginative freedom, gained no general support. It is arguable that if Irving had shown something of Garrick's adaptability, had acted the Professor for Barrie and Napoleon for Shaw, he might have prevented the public from falling into the error, from which it is only now beginning to recover, of supposing that the realistic convention is the only one that matters in the theatre. He might have shown those audiences—who, within their range, were responsive, excited, and theatre-wise—that there was a place in an actor's theatre for the dramatist, and in a dramatist's theatre for the great actor; and that realism and all the other -isms could exist side by side. But Irving was what he was, and this is mere conjecture. Irving and what he stood for went out of fashion, and the theatre became a sort of temple of realism.

Within its self-imposed limits, this Edwardian theatre, which may be said to have lasted till the outbreak of war in 1914, was an admirable theatre. Like the generation which it served, it was confident of its own rightness, and that every movement it made was forward. It had a keen and excited, though insular and intolerant, following of playgoers, who, wanting only one thing, were both

theatre-wise and discriminating where that one thing was concerned. In consequence, the characteristic of the time was a steady
improvement in technique and increase of range in the writers of
comedy, who, in the absence of any tragic or poetic writing for the
stage, found themselves expected to appeal to the deeper as well
as the more superficial emotions in their audiences. As a natural
result, the appeal to these deeper emotions was made less and less
directly; often their existence was merely presumed, while the
author's open appeal was to the heads rather than the hearts of
his audience. As the movement continued a place began to be
found in the theatre even for a satirist like Shaw. True, he was
irreverent in his attitude towards accepted institutions like marriage and doctors and war; but so long as it was understood that
he was no more than a mocker, who probably did not mean a word
he said, it had to be admitted that the fellow had brains, and was
amusing in a shocking way of his own.

Fashions in acting followed suit. It was the day of the light
comedian, the highly accomplished player with a delicate and
subtle touch, the type of actor which may be said to have culminated in Gerald du Maurier. If du Maurier happened to be playing
a part which ranked as serious (say, Sir Hubert Ware in *The Ware
Case*, a play which, though produced in 1915, was a very typical
example of this period of theatre history) he made no alteration
in his customary casual style. He had only to indicate by the
slightest of signs that under the mask of a well-brought-up English
gentleman he was suffering agonies of shame or remorse, and his
audience was more than ready to take those agonies for granted.
An old-fashioned audience would have expected him to express his
feelings openly and to the full—a task which would have been beyond him as an actor and repugnant to him as a realist. Du Maurier's audiences much preferred du Maurier's way; they left the
rather embarrassing method of direct emotional expression to the
small band of actors, all of them in the Irving tradition if not
actually of Irving's company or even of his blood, who still appeared as Hamlet with decreasing frequency and to lessening
applause—men like Martin Harvey, Matheson Lang, Forbes-
Robertson, H. B. Irving, and F. R. Benson. The old idea that
every young actor of high ambition should prove himself in this
most testing and most rewarding of all parts seemed to have
disappeared entirely. Post-war London audiences accepted Colin
Keith-Johnston in the part in 1924, but only because he played in

modern clothes, smoked a pipe, and kept to the realistic convention which they understood. Not until 1930, when Irving had been dead a quarter of a century, was any management rash enough to risk putting the play on for a West End run. Then at last, on the strength of John Gielgud's rising reputation gained on the unfashionable side of the river at the Old Vic, the experiment was tried; and its success seemed something in the order of a miracle. But more of that in its proper place. My concern for the moment is still with the Edwardian time, when Gielgud was a small child.

With the rise in the stage's social standing, and that loosening of rigid Puritan standards of behaviour which had come to the middle classes with increasing prosperity and more liberal education, there came a change in the quality of the recruits on which the theatre could draw. No longer was it necessary for stage-struck boys and girls 'of education and refinement' to brave an almost inevitable parental ban, and run away from their respectable homes to a life of vagabondage. They could join an academy founded by Tree under royal patronage and the most impressive auspices, or they could graduate from the ranks of the amateur societies; and though prejudice was an unconscionable time a-dying in some quarters, it could not alter the trend of events. Recruits of this new kind found a ready welcome on the stage because they had the breeding which fitted them for the new kind of play; and as the new dramatists grew more sure of themselves, they made demands on the rank and file of their players for acting of increasing intelligence and subtlety, and these demands were understood and met. That 'theatre of ideas', to which Shaw had pointed the way, seemed no longer a far-away dream; and in the prevailing mood of excitement about the future there were few to trouble their heads if the old-time theatre, whose first concern was not with the intellect but with the passions, had ceased to draw the public.

Among those few, naturally, were the actors and actresses of the old tradition, who found themselves dispossessed. Those who could learnt the new casual technique; those who could not adapt themselves grew crusty and disappointed, grumbling that the true artists of the stage had been ousted by a mob of ladies and gentlemen who knew how to behave, not how to act. Yet every now and then even these disgruntled players had their chances; for there was still a public, itself trained in the old school, ready to turn out to support, say, a Martin Harvey season at the Lyceum; and there were still occasions when some young leading lady was tried out as Juliet, or some actor-manager saw himself as Henry V. Such times, however, grew steadily fewer; and it is not too fanciful to say that the Old Drama had its swan-song with Forbes-Robertson's farewell performances in 1913, or that the New Drama reached its culmination with the emphatic success, in April 1914, of Shaw's *Pygmalion*. Then came the war, and with it this great theatrical period—for it *was* great, in its way—came to a sudden and fearful end.

Not that the theatres were closed overnight by order, as in World War II; not that anybody, in the theatre or out of it, realized at once that the period was over. The theatre struggled on in the old way for a little; it was the trained, theatre-wise audience that had vanished, and without it, for a time, the managers faced ruin. Then the new audience arrived—an untrained, undiscriminating horde of soldiers on leave and the girls they had left behind them, which formed a huge, ever-changing but never-failing floating population perpetually out on the spree. Their tastes were simple —they wanted noise, glitter, easy laughter, and if they could not find seats for one show they would go on to the next. In such circumstances the art of the theatre not merely could not flourish; it could barely exist. Here and there a good play was staged as if by accident—Barrie's *Dear Brutus*, for example—but one has only to look at the theatre advertisements in the files of the newspapers of that time to see how low the standard had dropped. In a book largely concerned with tracing the influences for good or bad which the condition of the public taste has upon the theatre which serves it, I could hardly find an example more striking or more melancholy.

Nor were matters much better when the war ended. Even when the hectic after-war excitement had died away, even when the American and Dominion armies had gone to their homes, even when London's floating population had dwindled to its usual peace-time size and composition, the fine self-confident audiences of early 1914 did not reassemble, or at any rate did not coalesce. The more sophisticated playgoers among them were in a bitter, disillusioned mood, the younger generation which had grown up in the disintegration of war was demoralized, while the main body of the public was beginning to find the cinema a powerful counter-attraction, and had lost some of its interest in the stage. Most of the leading serious dramatists of the Edwardian era were still writing, and some of them had much of their best work yet to

come. Pinero, once their leader, had fallen into a bewildered
silence which he was never again to break with effect; but Henry
Arthur Jones, Galsworthy, Somerset Maugham, and Barrie could
still draw audiences. Yet they could no longer count, as before,
on a homogeneous theatrical public which knew what it was about
and what it wanted. The clever people in the audiences, indeed,
seemed to take a delight in sneering at anything which did not fit
their world-weary mood; and I heard, in 1924, of a man who
described himself with pride to a theatre manager of my acquaintance as being 'one of the first-night "knockers" '. To such people
poetry was nonsense, and beauty, if looked at with a suitably jaun-
diced eye, could generally be dismissed as sentimentality. Only in
a mocking realism could they put any trust. Noel Coward's youthful and brilliant cynicism was exactly to their taste; and for their
more serious moments, there was Shaw.

For Shaw was now not simply one of the old brigade of dramatists, but an accredited major prophet. Long ago he had told
people, in *Arms and the Man*, that war was not a matter of brilliant
uniforms, romantic cavalry-skirmishes, and personal glory, but a
dirty, business-like affair in which transport mules counted for
more than chargers, and milk chocolate was often more important
than revolvers. He had been denounced as a liar; but now, as
everybody could see, it had turned out that he had known more
about soldiering than the soldiers themselves. Neither about war,
nor about women, nor about marriage, nor about medicine, nor
indeed about anything at all had he ever had any illusions; naturally, a disillusioned generation turned to him. Shaw took his
apotheosis—it was little less—rather uneasily. He had never much
liked it when people agreed with him, and to have quite so many
of them agreeing with him quite so much upset his idea of himself
as an advanced thinker. At first he was incredulous. In 1921, when
Charles Macdona asked for the right to send out a touring company
with a repertory of Shaw plays, the dramatist warned the manager
that he would ruin himself. Instead Macdona made a fortune, and
Shaw was compelled to adjust himself to the knowledge that his
plays were no longer shocking experiments but commercial assets.
His success was indeed phenomenal, and with the production of
Saint Joan in 1924 he took his place as the great theatrical figure
of his generation as unquestionably as Irving had taken it half a
century before.

William Archer, who with his own weapons had fought as hard

as Shaw—and for an immeasurably smaller reward—in the cause of the theatre of ideas, just lived to see that triumphant occasion, and must have felt it to be the culmination of his life's work. By that time he had retired from active criticism, having achieved financial independence at the age of sixty-seven by the success of his play *The Green Goddess* (which, by one of fate's quaintest ironies, was a piece of sheer melodrama, though certainly written in the realistic convention); and he had published in his last book, *The Old Drama and the New*, a firm statement of his belief in and satisfaction with the kind of theatre we had now got. It fell to my lot to review that book at considerable length in the *Daily Telegraph*, and, while treating it and its author with the respect which both deserved, I did take him to task for not allowing that other and very different kinds of theatre could, and ought to, exist side by side with his. Passages which I found particularly hard to swallow were one in which he suggested that the true line of development in the theatre lay 'away from Passion—that is to say, Passion for Passion's sake, Passion at all costs—towards ever more delicate and faithful Imitation'; and another in which he said that modern drama had 'cast out the foreign elements of rhetoric and lyricism, and become a pure art of interpretation through imitation', which purification 'is not a sign of degeneracy, but merely the last term of an inevitable and most desirable process of development'. When my shocked reaction to the last passage compelled me to accuse him of complacency, he replied with great good temper that he did not mean that modern realistic drama was perfect:

All I intended was a statement of strictly historical fact—that in the typical prose play (English and foreign) of the past thirty years a process of evolution had been consummated, and, on the mechanical or technical side, could no further go. How far it may go on the spiritual side I do not pretend to guess; and I admit theoretically, though I scarcely believe, that it may have landed us in a blind alley, from which the theatre may have to 'try back'.

It is significant that just as, at the beginning of his writing career, Archer took no account at all of the part played by the audience in a theatre, and denied that the actor who could make the spectator's blood run cold in his veins was 'even a passable actor' if he were without certain physical qualities, so at the end of his life he could argue about the future without taking into consideration the possibility—which is in fact a certainty—of changes in the public taste. Once having got rid, thankfully, of 'Passion for Passion's sake' (by which, in my view, he really meant great act-

F

ing) he cannot visualize a future in which audiences will be so wrong-headed, or so ungrateful, as to want it back again. And yet there was evidence to be had that an audience trained on passion for passion's sake was a more rewarding audience even for realistic plays than the theatre audience trained on such plays. When Irene Vanbrugh asked Barrie to let her take *The Twelve Pound Look* on the music halls, he at first refused, thinking his work would not appeal to big popular audiences. Relenting later, he found that the play actually went better in the London Hippodrome than in the regular theatre, and that he actually preferred the music-hall audience, with its direct, hearty expression of its opinions, to the politer but less inspiring theatre audience. If Archer had pondered on that evidence he might have seen, being as he was an exceptionally fair-minded man, that the people who were capable of appreciating *The Twelve Pound Look* at the Hippodrome were potential playgoers who had been driven from the theatre by its arid addiction to his favourite formula, 'ever more delicate and faithful Imitation'. These people had no special objection to realism as such, but they wanted something more. They also wanted 'the foreign elements of rhetoric and lyricism'; in a word, they wanted passion for passion's sake, and because they could get it in the music hall (admittedly, in a crude form) and could not get it in the theatre, to the music hall they went, and left the theatre the poorer for their loss. Archer, however, did not think theatrically. He thought in terms of the written drama, and of actors and playhouses as adjuncts to the business of giving the play a three-dimensional form. And so he died happy in the belief that the dramatist had at last been given a theatre in which he could and would go on and on writing better and better plays, for more and more intellectually appreciative audiences. But it was not to work out like that. Within ten years of Archer's death the invention of the talking film had enticed a whole generation away from the living theatre, while the rise of an English school of ballet and the amazing success of its performances had shown clearly that there was a strong contingent, even among the faithful, who preferred that the theatre should appeal to the senses rather than to the intellect. All over the country playhouses were closing down or being converted into cinemas. The provincial theatre had practically ceased to exist except in a few big towns; and in London the dramatists, under the increasingly sure and confident lead of J. B. Priestley, were making experiments both in the form and in the content of their plays in an attempt to recapture, or at any rate to replace, those elements of rhetoric and lyricism on which Archer had triumphantly written sentence of perpetual banishment.

Meanwhile Shaw, having established a supremacy never before held by a dramatist in the whole history of our theatre, and having attained a degree of technical skill in writing for the stage which enabled him to play any tricks with his medium that suited his fancy, proceeded to prove himself what Gordon Craig has called him, 'a sincere enemy to the theatre'. He declared war quite openly in the Fifth Part of *Back to Methuselah*, first produced at Birmingham in 1923. In that play, you remember, humanity has contrived to extend its span of life almost indefinitely, and it is therefore living Shaw's conception of the perfect life. In that life, a new human creature is born full-grown from an egg—not a bad idea at all—and has just four years in which to work off its appetites for sex and beauty and art. It then dries up into a sexless Ancient, and spends thousands and thousands of years in solitary contemplation. Whether this would really be much fun we need not consider here; my point is that this shows us Shaw's true opinion of the theatre—an amusement for undeveloped creatures, not worth an adult's time. Feeling so, and finding himself all the same in command of the citadel, he next proceeded to undermine it from within and to try to blow it up. In other words, from *Back to Methuselah* onwards he was engaged in a continuous attempt to turn the theatre into something which it could not be, namely, a debating platform or lecture hall.

In *Saint Joan* he succeeded, so far as he went, but for reasons outside himself. The story of Joan of Arc is a great one in itself, and Shaw found himself bound not only to tell that story, but to keep it within its historical framework. The result was that when he let himself go in intellectual exposition, once in the magnificent Tent Scene and again when the Inquisitor sets forth Joan's situation in the last act, the long speeches were part of the story and had the right theatrical feel about them. They made Joan's death at the stake seem inevitable to the audience in almost exactly the same way as Oedipus's equally innocent offence against taboos of which he did not know the existence made his tragic end seem inevitable. That is to say that Saint Joan was the nearest thing to a tragic part for a great actress that Shaw ever wrote, or that anybody wrote during the Shaw era. But having stated his tragic theme intellectually, Shaw runs away theatrically from its climax. He avoids passion because he does not feel it; and the end of the play, clever and characteristic though it is, may well be merely the author's escape from a part of his story which demands an emotional power that is not in him.

At any rate, he never gave tragedy another chance to creep up on him. More and more, in those last plays which he wrote for successive festivals in his honour at Malvern, he used the dramatic form merely as a convenient method for assembling a group of characters round a table (or, as in *The Apple Cart*, across the stage in a row like a company of Christy Minstrels), and letting them talk each other down. That the talk was brilliant at its best and never dull even at its worst is nothing to the point. Shaw, paramount in the theatre, was treating the theatre with contempt, and I believe that in time to come the theatre will revenge itself for his treachery by neglecting all his later plays—even, it may be, *Saint Joan* itself.

What of the actors during this time? As actors must, they gave their public the kind of acting that it would accept. Recruitment from the more highly educated sections of the community increased steadily, for after the war the dramatic societies of the universities all over the country began to take themselves with a new seriousness as possible training-grounds for young men and women who wanted to go on the stage. In a theatre devoted to the intelligence this was a very acceptable development, and very soon it was possible to boast that the standard of rank-and-file acting on our stage had never been higher. On the other hand, no generation of players had ever been compelled to confine its command of the actor's art within narrower limits. Nothing was required of them but Archer's 'ever more delicate and faithful Imitation', and soon it was regarded as heresy in any actor even to wish to act in any other style. Those who felt they needed more breadth, and took the occasional opportunities to appear in classic revivals, found themselves suspect. If they continued in their heterodox behaviour, they were labelled 'Shakespearean' and, regarded as belonging to a race apart, were no longer in the running for parts in modern plays.

An excellent example of the kind of thing that was happening is to be found in the career of Godfrey Tearle. Born as he was of a theatrical family, and having taken professionally to the stage (in 1899) at the age of fifteen, he had been trained in the old style on the classical repertory and was an all-round actor, equally at home in doublet and hose or a lounge suit. Coming back to the stage from the army, he played the lead in a very successful modern play, *The Garden of Allah*, and followed it up with a performance of Othello which lives in my memory to this day and in which, if I have any power of judgement at all, he touched greatness. If that performance had been given before audiences of discrimination and wide experience it would have been recognized as something outstanding, and would have led to a public demand that the same actor should be seen in other big classical parts. There was no such demand, and a few months later Tearle appeared in a modern thriller. It was eleven years before he appeared again in any Shakespeare play for a run, and this in spite of the fact that once, being cast for Horatio in an all-star special performance of *Hamlet*, it was he rather than the Hamlet (Henry Ainley) who dominated the stage whenever they were on together. That *tour de force* did indeed cause something of a stir, but it was not enough to bring about the rescue of one of the finest emotional actors of our time from his task of impersonating a series of virile nitwits in plays of no importance.

Contrast with this the career of Sybil Thorndike. Actually a little older than Tearle, she came to the stage later than he did and was not known in London before the war. She first made her name at the Old Vic during the war years, and so wore the dangerous Shakespearean label almost from the beginning. She, too, touched greatness with performances as Hecuba in *The Trojan Women* and as Medea, given at special matinées before the few audiences that had enough experience to appreciate plays so far removed from the events of everyday England. In her case a public demand was made that she should show what she could do in modern drama, and so, in order to qualify as a London leading lady, she played in a round of sensational parts in a *Grand Guignol* season at the Little Theatre, soon after appeared as a film star in a satirical piece called *Advertising April*, and later on in Henry Arthur Jones's *The Lie*. The classical label still stuck to her, however, and it was almost with a sigh of relief that the public heard that she was to play Joan of Arc for Shaw. Since the play was by Shaw it was bound to be modern in treatment, and since Miss Thorndike was to be Saint Joan she could be as 'period' as she liked; a very happy arrangement all round.

How well she played that part has been becoming more and more clear as time goes on, and other well-graced actresses fail to dim one's memory of her performance. Yet at the time it hardly seemed that she had done full justice to the opportunity. The evening was a triumph for Mr Shaw, there was no doubt about that; and a success?—oh, yes, certainly quite a success for Miss Thorndike. Now it is becoming clear that the fault that her success was not greater lay with Shaw, for Joan is not a great acting part. For one thing, it breaks in two; the rough peasant lass of the early part of the play and the ecstatic saint-to-be of the later scenes are not really the same person. Shaw knew nothing about peasant lasses and was not interested in them, but he knew a great deal about saints. About Joan the village girl, then, he wrote perfunc- torily from without; about the saint, sympathetically from within. Because he failed to fuse the two, no actress has managed to do so. Hardly an actress has tried, except Sybil Thorndike. Again, if Joan is to be a great acting part, the tragic figure she could be, she must carry the climax of the play; but Shaw's climax comes when Joan is at the stake in Rouen market-place, off the stage, and the actress is in her dressing-room. When she returns for the Epilogue the air is no longer charged with emotion, nor is she; her mood is one of Shavian mockery, a deliberate anti-climax and a turning away from sublimity. It may be said that Shaw wrote the play as he liked and had every right to do so. Exactly so; but the actress must not be asked to shoulder the blame when he fails her, especi- ally if he fails her on purpose.

So far as the general playgoing public of the 1920's was con- cerned, then, the whole of the great English acting tradition might have vanished overnight and nobody would have cared. The tradition was not lost, however. Even in those dark days it was possible for the enthusiast to see the classics well acted, if he knew where to look. He could join Sunday societies, or he could see Nigel Playfair's work at Hammersmith, or he could become a fre- quenter of the Old Vic. This most remarkable theatre of our time has had its history discussed too often for me to add to the tale; here I am concerned chiefly with its audience. This was drawn from all over London, and often from farther afield; and it con- sisted of people who were prepared to take a little extra trouble, when they went to the theatre, to seek out the kind of plays and the kind of acting that they liked in the only place where it was then to be found. They were not very numerous, but there were enough of them to keep one big theatre reasonably well filled night after night. Their very existence seemed impossible to the cynics of the West End, and any suggestion that people could go to the Waterloo Road for enjoyment was dismissed as naïve. Obviously, said the cynics when the Old Vic audience began to earn a fame of its own, these people were pretending to enjoy themselves in order to make a sort of 'clique' reputation as superior persons. This suggestion was of course completely false, but the fact that it could be made throws a lurid light on the kind of people who made it.

In fact, that Old Vic audience was the only theatrically intelligent audience in the London of its time; alert, responsive, immeasurably quicker than the West End to pick up an acting point, and consequently a joy to play to. Very soon, actors and actresses were paying large sums for the privilege of playing to it—paying not in cash, of course, but in the sacrifice of contracts to play elsewhere at very much higher salaries. Lilian Baylis's famous prayer to God to send her good actors and let her have them cheap was answered in the most direct way, for almost any ambitious young actor was prepared to become a cheap actor when an engagement to play leads at the Old Vic was in question. And hardly a player who bought himself this experience ever had reason to regret it, for the improvement in his work from the moment he appeared before this audience was astonishing. Actors like John Gielgud, Laurence Olivier, Ralph Richardson, Roger Livesey; actresses like Edith Evans, Flora Robson, Ursula Jeans were seen to increase their power and range almost week by week under its evocative influence.

It would be inaccurate as well as ungracious to give all the credit for the rise of this younger generation of fine actors to the audiences. Every one of the successive producers—Ben Greet, Russell Thorndike, Robert Atkins, Andrew Leigh, Harcourt Williams—who built up the theatre's tradition during the first world war and kept it going during the spiritually barren 1920's must have his share, as well as the many good players of the older school who led the early teams. But without audiences of special quality their efforts might well have failed, and certainly would not have had the far-reaching influence which was theirs in the end. As time went on and the fame of the Old Vic increased, the scoffers of the West End fell silent and began to wonder uneasily whether they were not, after all, missing something good. Some of them, to whom the Waterloo Road had seemed as distant as the Hebrides, made experimental journeys and found it was hardly farther away from the centre of things than Drury Lane itself. Then, in 1929, John Gielgud appeared for the first time as Hamlet; and the motor-cars stood in line for the Old Vic as once, nearly two hundred years before, the coaches had stood in line for Goodman's Fields.

There is no suggestion here that in Gielgud we had found, or could ever find, a new Garrick. If only for physical reasons, Gielgud is not in the line of the great actors; he is not strong enough. To quote the phrase he uses of himself in his autobiography, he has 'not enough virility' for the soldier heroes, Othello or Macbeth, and he lacks the final ounce or two of power for Lear. But he seems to have been born to play Hamlet and, within the limitations of his own conception, he played it exquisitely. I have never seen a better Hamlet, and hardly dare hope that I ever can, yet it made no attempt at greatness. The actor was enough product of his own time to be afraid of the theatrical values of the part, though he faced its spiritual values squarely. It was said with approval at the time that he played the part 'unselfishly', which means that he made Hamlet a leading character in the play rather than its heart's core. It was in line with his reticent way of playing that when, later, he produced the play himself, he lifted the curtain on the first court scene with Hamlet so tucked away in the shadows that the spectators had to search about to make sure he was on the stage at all. This was hardly the high tragic idea, but it was indicative of an engaging modesty, and was quite possibly the only kind of Hamlet which spectators trained in the realistic school of team-acting could have been persuaded to accept. At all events, they did accept it. The Old Vic company played a season in the West End in the following year, 1930, and so put an end to the state of heathen blindness into which the general playgoing public had allowed itself to sink. The appeal of that particular Hamlet to that particular public lay not only in its sensibility, but its sense. Gielgud's avoidance of self-assertion made sense of Hamlet's irresoluteness, his extraordinary faculty for speaking verse as if it were the expression of his own immediate thought made sense of an unfamiliar medium. No other actor at that time could have brought poetic beauty back to the London theatre, and the full glory of the achievement must always be his.

Other signs were not lacking that the trend of the public taste was rising, or rather broadening, during the 1930's. Although classical tragedy, even after Gielgud's success in *Hamlet*, still had only a precarious hold on the public attention, it was noticeable that any actors who showed signs of an emotional equipment beyond the average quickly gained a following, and that strong, bold acting in classical comedy—such as was shown, for instance, by Edith Evans as Lady Bracknell in *The Importance of Being Earnest*—was received with joy. Though Charles Laughton, after making a great reputation, gave up the theatre for the films, a dozen names come easily to mind of young men and women who in those years were acclaimed for performances which gave the passions full play. Actresses like Peggy Ashcroft, Flora Robson, Wendy Hiller, and actors like Ralph Richardson, Laurence Olivier, Wilfrid Lawson, Raymond Massey, Robert Morley, Emlyn Williams or Donald Wolfit showed that if the audience was willing once again to have its heart wrung, the actor was still able to wring it. And there were encouraging signs that, in spite of the competition of the talking pictures, a new and less narrow-minded theatrical public was being born. The amateur movement was by now in full swing, and in every part of the country theatre-lovers were learning by practical personal experience something of the actor and his art. There are some, I know, who say that the amateur movement contributes little to the theatre as a whole, since its tendency too often is to produce in the amateur a complacent interest in his own doings which makes him a worse instead of a better playgoer. There is truth in this for I have come across amateurs who consider that none but the very best professionals have anything to show them, and will hardly condescend to enter a theatre as a result. Even so, the presence in the community of a large body of informed opinion about the theatre must raise the standard of responsiveness in the end.

More important even than the amateur movement, however, was the growing interest in the drama shown by the schools, with every encouragement, under successive Governments of different political views, from the Board—and later the Ministry—of Education. Children who had grown up to think of acting as something that was done by a photographic image on a screen were introduced to the idea of live players and non-realistic plays before they were old enough to have developed prejudices; and some of the school productions which I saw in steadily increasing numbers during the 1930's rank among my most rewarding adventures in playgoing. It seemed certain that when these children grew up they would form a playgoing generation more emotionally receptive and less intellectually hidebound than their fathers had been, and would give the actors a chance to cultivate the whole field of their art instead of only a corner.

Chapter 14

THE THEATRE IN CONVALESCENCE

WHEN WAR WAS DECLARED AGAINST GERMANY FOR THE SECOND time, and every theatre in the country was closed by order of the Government, nobody could make even the wildest kind of guess when, or in what conditions, any form of acting would begin again. London and all the big cities lay under the immediate threat of being bombed, and until the measure of that threat had been taken there could be no question of 'business as usual'. In the event, a surprising amount of theatre work was done up and down the country in the first twenty months of the war, before the Germans recognized the failure of their air attacks and their plans for invasion, and in that time London ceased, for the first time in her history, to be the headquarters of the English stage. She became a place to which theatre companies might pay fleeting visits when either the lightening of the German attacks, or the hours of performance, permitted. In stage terms, London had become a 'touring date'; and not until after the last severe bombing raid, on 10 May 1941, did she become once more the home of the long run.

When at last the West End returned to a condition that could be referred to without much irony as 'normal', and became again, as in the first war, the resort of the soldier on leave, those who cared for the art of the theatre prepared, with heavy hearts, to see the standard of the public taste dive steeply to the depths which it had reached in 1916 and after. No such thing happened. It soon became clear that a playgoing population which was, or might at any moment be, in immediate danger of death had an attitude to its playgoing quite different from that of a public outside the area of acute danger; it was willing, and at times, eager, to face truth. Naturally, it had a liking for light, gay pieces, but it did not close its mind to serious or unhappy things as the London public of the former world war had insisted on doing, with a frenzied escapism that had lasted far into the 1920's and had helped to keep down the artistic standards of that unhappy period.

Two plays may be used to illustrate this point. The first is

Emlyn Williams's *The Morning Star*. This piece was written immediately after the bombing of London had been abandoned, and was
the expression of Williams's deep admiration for the behaviour of
his adopted city and its people. Writing at white heat, he seemed
not to have troubled his head very much about a plot for his play,
for its actual story was not impressive. All the emphasis was on the
simple, unemphatic heroism of the characters when the bombs fell.
Knowing that such a play produced during or after the first war
would have met with instant disaster, and expecting no better fate,
Williams still wished his tribute to be placed on record. To his
astonishment (as his face showed when he bowed his acknowledge-
ments to the applause on the first night) the play was a great popular success, running for nearly five hundred performances. The
date of the production was 10 December 1941; and the fact that
the nerves of London playgoers were so steady that they could
listen to imitation bomb-explosions less than six months after they
had heard the real thing was indeed astonishing.

The second play I have in mind was Terence Rattigan's *Flare
Path*, an Air Force play, light enough in texture but with an under-
lying seriousness of intention, giving a realistic picture of the life
of carefully hidden anxiety and terror lived by the wives and sweet-
hearts of the bomber crews. This was accepted by the public with
even greater satisfaction than the other, for it ran for over six
hundred and fifty performances. It is significant that when these
plays reached New York, which was in the struggle yet outside the
danger area, as London had been in the first war, and consequently
was in the same obstinately escapist frame of mind, both were rejected out of hand on the ground that they were very bad plays.
In the case of *The Morning Star* such criticism was justifiable, since
the particular reason for which it had been written, and for which
London had liked it, had no validity in American eyes. *Flare Path*,
on the other hand, was a good enough play to have been given its
chance of success if Americans had been in a mood to take it. That
they were not in a mood to take it was due merely to the geographi-
cal accident that they were not a part of the battlefield.

All England, even the areas regarded as comparatively safe, *was*
a part of the battlefield, and as a consequence the same readiness
to like serious entertainment had manifested itself in the provinces,
which by this time were the scenes of extraordinary theatrical
activity. The value of organized entertainment as a way of keeping
up morale in the forces and output in the factories had been well

established in the first world war, and in the second was recognized from the start. 'E.N.S.A.' was brought back into existence to supply plays and other shows to the services on a tremendous scale, and in addition entertainment officers were appointed to make arrangements for various individual formations. A multiplicity of private ventures came into being to do a similar service for the war-workers, and eventually the need grew so great that the Government took a hand, and established the Council for the Encouragement of Music and the Arts as a co-ordinating and directing body with some public money at its disposal. This work done by C.E.M.A. was so valuable that the organization was later made permanent and given a larger subsidy, and under the new name of the Arts Council of Great Britain had functions which in other countries generally fall in the sphere of a Ministry of Fine Arts.

Side by side with these developments which, though cultural in their effects, were caused by the necessity to carry the war to success, came a renaissance of the ordinary provincial theatre which was much more accidental in origin. Immense numbers of people from the big towns had been evacuated to smaller, safer towns. Before the war, these people had formed the great bulk of the play-going public, and they took their tastes and demands to their temporary homes. Great Government departments moved bodily out, and proceeded to grow still greater. Theatre managers who were debarred for the moment from London were quick to see the opportunity this gave them, and in a very short time the touring system, which had dropped dead ten years before with the arrival of the talking film, had been revived. Theatres which had then been converted into picture houses were in some cases reconverted to their original use.

One way and another, Britain's theatrical fare about the middle of the war and onwards was fine confused feeding. Every kind of show was being offered to every kind of audience. Mistakes were made, of course, and complaints were heard. On the one hand it was suggested that our citizen armies were being given entertainment suited only to the brutal and licentious soldiery of legend, and on the other, that there was too much Euripides about; but it became noticeable that while the former complaint was usually made by the soldiers themselves, the latter came more often than not from pessimistic theorists. As time went on, such theorists fell into a surprised silence as it became clear that in forces, factories and civil life alike a new theatrical public had come into being, and that its tastes were both broader and higher than those of the regular playgoing public between the wars. The way in which I should myself prefer to explain what had happened is that the younger generation, after a period in which it had been led astray in the wilderness, had been given a chance to re-discover the theatre. For some of this generation the way for discovery had been prepared at school; but for many, it was as exciting a novelty to see flesh-and-blood actors playing on real stages as it had been for their fathers to see moving images acting out a story on a screen. For different reasons, neither of these kinds of newcomers to the theatre had any special prejudice in favour of the realistic convention. Poetry was as easily acceptable to them as prose, and they were ready to respond to direct, undisguised emotion without embarrassment.

This change of temper in the audiences must have been going on for some time before its effects were clearly discernible. Perhaps the first real evidence that things were taking a turn for the better came from Stratford-on-Avon, where year by year the Shakespeare Memorial Theatre played to larger and more eager audiences; but if so, the real significance of Shakespeare's greater popularity was not seen till later. At the time it was put down to the fact that Stratford was a favourite playground and leave-centre for the American armies. When these armies left for home after the end of the war, confident and gloomy prophets said that the Stratford audiences would dwindle away; but instead they increased. Meanwhile in London, though it was always very noticeable that there were no signs of any degradation of public taste and that plays of a good standard could safely be put on, the increasing catholicity of the audience was not clearly recognized until the middle of 1943, when it became obvious that John Gielgud's revival of Congreve's *Love for Love* was settling down to be a popular success on a scale that seemed quite fantastic.

The piece had been presented, as most revivals of little-known classics are presented, rather because the actor wanted to stage it than because the public was expected to visit it in great numbers. Indeed, so clearly was it aimed at a comparatively small, sophisticated public that the management did not care to risk what was considered a certain, though not great, loss of money on it, and produced it as a non-profit-making venture under the ægis of the C.E.M.A. Yet it ran well over a year, and made vast profits which, by the rules of the game, could not be distributed and had to be used to finance other 'unprofitable' ventures which also showed a strange tendency to popularity. Nothing like this had happened in the West End of London for many years, or indeed could have happened at any time between the two wars. There were still a few determined cynics who explained away the long run of *Love for Love* on the ground that its incidental indecency had hit the taste of a demoralized war-time generation, but these had their answer in the following year when Laurence Olivier and Ralph Richardson were released from the Fleet Air Arm to become joint directors of the Old Vic Company in its tenure of the New Theatre, and drew delighted crowds to see such blameless but uncomfortable classics as Ibsen's *Peer Gynt* and Chekhov's *Uncle Vanya*, together with Shaw's *Arms and the Man* and Shakespeare's *King Richard III*.

Although the choice of plays shows that what the directors originally had in mind was to form a strong repertory company which, by playing constantly together in a variety of plays, should develop in a high degree the modern virtue of team-work, the new spirit of the times was too much for them; for in *Richard III* Olivier gave a performance in the old grand manner which had been out of favour for a generation, and was received with acclamation great enough to begin a new chapter in theatrical history. Richard Crookback has always been a favourite character with actors ever since Cibber restored it to the repertory in his own garbled version in 1700; that version held the stage for one hundred and twenty years, and Shakespeare's original, restored by Macready in 1821, has had an equally firm hold on the public ever since. Because Richard is a self-confessed villain who constantly takes the audience into his confidence, the play defies realistic production and therefore, with the coming of the Shaw era, was not among the small number of classics which West End audiences could then be expected to stand. With the less hide-bound audiences at the Old Vic and Stratford, however, it continued to be greatly popular, and even in those lean years dramatic critics and others whose playgoing was regular and comprehensive saw this play acted again and again, and particularly well acted by Baliol Holloway.

Many a time, then, I had seen Richard limp down the stage to speak his opening lines:

> Now is the winter of our discontent
> Made glorious summer by this sun of York. . . .

which make the simplest and yet somehow one of the most effec-

tive beginnings to a play ever invented. But I had never seen any
Richard do what Olivier did—make of it an elaborate stage
entrance worthy to be set beside Irving's entrance in *The Bells* as
Craig describes it. He came in at the back, and made his progress
down-stage a thing of so many artfully contrived but deeply significant pauses and hesitations, of so much play of expression, that it
seemed as if the time that elapsed before he spoke could be reckoned
by minutes rather than seconds. It was so deliberate a use of stage
methods to make a stage effect that I believe one of the 'hard-
boiled' audiences of the 'twenties would have broken into nervous
titters at the sight of it. But before the first line was delivered the
actor had told us so much about the man he was impersonating
that he had me (and, I could feel, the rest of the audience) sitting
forward, tensely attentive and quite certain that I was about to see
the best Richard of my experience. And after the first speech I
could, if it had been necessary, have written a notice. Olivier had
done what Garrick had done in his day—thought this part out
freshly in the light of his own nature, Richard's nature, and the
nature of the playhouse, and had given a performance which was
at once highly theatrical and, in the best and truest sense of the
word, completely natural. What was more, Olivier had had the
good fortune which Garrick also in his day had had, to find an
audience ready to respond to him.

Once assured of the quality of their audience, the actors of the
Old Vic Company could go forward in confidence. In the next
season it was Richardson's turn to show that Shakespeare could
once again be played in the grand manner, by playing Falstaff in
both parts of *King Henry IV*, and incidentally showing us how much
this magnificent play loses if, as usually happens, one half of it is
produced without reference to the other. Falstaff is perhaps the
only comic character in the whole range of drama which demands
as much from the player as the great tragic parts; it can only be
made effective by an actor with enough authority and power to
take it in his stride, without visible straining to be fat or funny. But
an actor who can do this has no difficulty in carrying an audience
with him, for Falstaff is himself an endearing rascal who com-
mands our sympathy without an effort. Therefore, the delight of
the public in Richardson's playing of the fat knight, though a
deserved tribute to the actor, cannot be produced as evidence of
any special degree of perceptiveness in the audience. But when that
same public paid to Olivier's Oedipus the tribute of rapt attention

and deep emotional response, then it became possible to believe without reserve that great days in the theatre might once again be in store for us. This belief was confirmed the following season, when Olivier's equally 'natural', original, and unexpectedly tender playing of Lear was received with applause which might almost have caused Gordon Craig, if he had been there, to admit that the house had been brought down for the first time since Irving's day.

Elsewhere the same tale was being told. I have already mentioned the strong tide that set in year after year towards Stratford, which maintained itself in spite of the inaccessibility of Shakespeare's town except by road, and the difficulty, accentuated rather than relieved by the end of the war, of using that particular means of approach. All through these years, also, Donald Wolfit, an actor who had devoted himself almost entirely to the classics, had proved ever more clearly both in London and in the provinces that vigorous, imaginative, and above all emotional acting had an irresistible appeal.

What I have said above constitutes no more than a sketch in outline, but so far as it goes I believe that it gives a true picture of our theatre as it is at the moment when these words are being written; and if so, it shows that we are in the presence of a great opportunity. During the writing of this book I have convinced myself, if nobody else, that the only foundation for a live and worthwhile theatre is a live and worth-while audience; and such an audience we have to-day. It is an audience with the supreme virtue of catholicity of taste, fit and able to mend the unfortunate rift between the theatre of the passions and the theatre of the intellect which began in Irving's day and has gone on widening ever since. It is an audience which can see no reason why it should not enjoy Shakespeare one day and Shaw the next, and its readiness to respond to, and ability to accept, almost any convention in which an author may choose to write means that the actor can work in a new atmosphere of understanding and sympathy whether he is wearing a lounge suit or doublet and hose.

In the presence of such an audience, the arid highbrow finds himself put to disconcerted silence. His pretence that the loftiest and noblest kind of theatre is a theatre of the brain is seen to be nonsense, and in its place comes a general understanding that theatrical art is a popular art, and that therefore even in its highest manifestations it must have a popular appeal—that a really great play will never go above the heads of the general public. To the intellectuals, this means that the aim of drama must always be disgracefully low, since the highest common intelligence factor of a large audience can never be impressive enough to cope with any but the simplest intellectual problems. For the man of the theatre this difficulty does not arise. He may, like Ibsen, be very much of an intellectual himself, but still he knows that any intellectual appeal made to a theatre audience must be incidental, and so, in the last resort, does not matter. The intellectual appeal in *A Doll's House*, for instance, was to people who were interested in the emancipation of women. Women were emancipated long ago, yet still the play keeps its stage appeal, because what really mattered to Ibsen when he was writing the play, and what still matters to the audience which sees it acted, is not Woman but a woman, Nora Helmer, who turns to her husband in her distress and finds that he has failed her.

The true theatre-man understands, further, that if he can appeal to the hearts of his auditors he welds them into a single entity, an audience, while if he addresses himself to their heads he splits them up into unrelated or even mutually antagonistic groups. *Hamlet* is the best example here. By common consent, it is the finest serious play in our language, and few would suggest that it has no intellectual appeal. To the intellectual, indeed, it presents a whole mass of problems and inconsistencies, which are material for endless disputation; but approached by way of the passions it is utterly simple—simple enough, indeed, to have been made into a successful film. More than any other play in the language, it enables the actor to establish emotional accord in his audience, and between himself and his audience. The intellectual, if he is wise as well as clever, responds to the actor's emotional appeal while he is in the theatre, and keeps his arguments about how old Hamlet is, and how mad, and why the tedious Polonius suddenly talks so brilliantly to his departing son, and how much Gertrude knew of Claudius's doings, and other deeper questionings, till afterwards. Ibsen's plays, dreary though most of them can seem, are alive to-day because when it came to the point Ibsen always sank the social reformer in the dramatist, and put his story and his characters before the lesson they were designed to teach.

One great hope for the future of our theatre is the fact that not only the audiences and the actors but the best of our practising dramatists now realize the paramount importance of the emotional approach in serious plays. Emlyn Williams's *The Wind of Heaven* may be taken as one example, but perhaps not the most striking, since Williams, as an actor and a Welshman, may be presumed to be more emotional in himself than other dramatists. A better proof is found in the first really serious play by Terence Rattigan (a master of stage technique), *The Winslow Boy*. In this play Rattigan is as much of a social reformer as Ibsen, and proves himself as complete a man of the theatre. His aim is to protest at the tendency to-day of Government departments to override the claims of individual citizens, and he does it by means of a close paraphrase of the famous Archer-Shee case. Here is a chance for intellectual argument which no dramatist of the Shaw Era could have missed. Rattigan avoided it completely, even to the point of allowing a trial scene—usually regarded as a gift to any dramatist—to take place off-stage. He presented the whole case, not as a *cause célèbre* but as the story of a family's courage, self-sacrifice, and eventual hard-won victory in the face of injustice. The result was a triumphantly successful play. When the curtain fell on the first-night performance I heard, more clearly than at any other such occasion of recent years, that note of unreserved enthusiasm which no audience can produce unless it has given itself absolutely, not in surrender but in co-operation.

If the tried and tested dramatists know how to turn to account the new responsiveness of their audiences, it should be possible to take for granted that the younger ones will know this too, since they are themselves part of the new movement and have grown up with it. About this, however, there is little tangible evidence yet, for although the war has been over a long time now there are still, as I write, hardly any new dramatists of any seriousness. The best of them, Peter Ustinov, certainly does make his appeal direct to the emotions and only incidentally to the intellect, but Ustinov, like Emlyn Williams, is an actor, and may not be typical. The great expense of putting on plays makes managers reluctant or unable to risk failure with the work of untried authors, and till some solution of this problem is found we shall not know the shape of plays to come. What that solution will be this is not the place to speculate; and a temporary lack of young serious dramatists, though deeply disappointing, is not fatal to the theatre's progress. We have the audience and we have the actors; and we have shelves full of fine plays with which they can tide over the time until the dramatists arrive.

Even so, in a world of shifting and uncertain values I must not end on a note of undue optimism, or appear to think that we are now on an upward spiral which will carry us, logically and inevitably, into a great theatrical period. I should be very sorry to commit myself to any prophecy so precise, or so rash, as that. What I do think is that we have a chance, such as we never had between the wars, of swinging into such a period. I feel that our Theatre at this moment is in a state of happy convalescence after a long and severe illness, and that it depends on many external circumstances whether recovery is to be complete and triumphant or partial and anxious. But at least the poison is eradicated—that overdose of intellectualism which Shaw injected in the firm belief that he had discovered the elixir of life.

BIBLIOGRAPHY

Chapter 3

Essay on Dramatic Poesie, 1668, by John Dryden.
Apology for the Life of Mr Colley Cibber, Comedian, 1740, by Colley
  Cibber.

Chapters 4 and 5

The Life of David Garrick, 1801, by Arthur Murphy.
Memoirs of the Life of David Garrick, 1805, by Thomas Davies.
Memoirs, 1806–7, by Richard Cumberland.
Memoirs, by Tate Wilkinson.
Lichtenberg's Visits to England, 1938, translated and annotated by
  Margaret L. Mare and W. H. Quarrell.

Chapters 6 and 7

Life of Mrs Siddons, 1834, by Thomas Campbell.
Memoirs of Mrs Siddons, 1896, by James Boaden.
The Kembles, 1871, by P. H. Fitzgerald.
Records of a Girlhood, 1878, by Frances Anne Kemble.
Mrs Siddons, 1887, by Mrs Arthur Kennard.

Chapters 8 and 9

Life and Enterprises of R. W. Elliston, 1857, by George Raymond.
Collected Works of William Hazlitt, 1902–4.
Edmund Kean, 1933, by Harold Newcomb Hillebrand.
Kean, 1939, by Giles Playfair.

Chapters 10 and 11

The Life of Sir Henry Irving, 1908, by Austin Brereton
Personal Reminiscences of Sir Henry Irving, 1908, by Bram Stoker.
The Story of My Life, 1908, by Ellen Terry.
Henry Irving, 1930, by Edward Gordon Craig.
The Garrick Club, 1948, by Guy Boas.
The Diaries of William Charles Macready, 1833–51, 1912, edited by
  William Toynbee.

Chapter 13

The Old Drama and the New, 1923, by William Archer

Index